zotero for genealogy

The Golden Egg Genealogist Series

Golden Egg Genealogists™ (GEGs) are marked by an ambition to excellence in the pursuit of their ancestry. Perpetually on their way to a better self, they know the treasures of genealogy offer themselves to the worthy. See gegbound.com for details.

zotero for genealogy

Harnessing the Power of Your Research

DONNA COX BAKER

Golden Channel Publishing
TUSCALOOSA, ALABAMA

Published in the United States of America by Golden Channel Publishing, Tuscaloosa, Alabama.

First Edition 2019

Cover design by the author. CC0 public domain image courtesy Max Pixel at https://www.maxpixel.net/Fantasy-Waterfall-Mystical-Woman-Desert-Mill-Mood-2820091.

Zotero is a project of the Corporation for Digital Scholarship and the Roy Rosenzweig Center for History and New Media at George Mason University. It was initially funded by the Andrew W. Mellon Foundation, the Institute of Museum and Library Services, and the Alfred P. Sloan Foundation. This book is not a publication of any of the above institutions. It is, however, produced with the permission of the Roy Rosenzweig Center for History and New Media.

Zotero is a trademark of the Corporation for Digital Scholarship. The Golden Egg Genealogist and Golden Channel Publishing are trademarked terms of Golden Channel Publishing.

ZotFile is an add-on freeware tool programmed by Joscha Legewie. His project is maintained at http://zotfile.com/.

Evidence Explained: Citing History Sources from Artifacts to Cyberspace, Third Edition, revised (2017) *(EE)*, by Elizabeth Shown Mills, is a publication of Genealogical Publishing Company of Baltimore, Maryland. The examples borrowed from *EE* are for educational purposes. The *EE*-to-Zotero method taught in this text is the creation of Donna Cox Baker and does not suggest the endorsement of *EE*'s author, publisher, or organization. Images

ISBN 978-0-9996899-1-2

Library of Congress Catalog Number: 2019900522

Golden Channel Publishing
6552 Ash Hill Drive
Tuscaloosa, Alabama 35405

goldenchannelpublishing.com

Visit our website and forum at
zoteroforgenealogy.com

For Mac and the babies

TABLE OF CONTENTS

Table of contents ix
Acknowledgments xiii
Preface xv
1: Introduction to Zotero for genealogy 1
What is Zotero? 2
How does Zotero serve genealogists? 3
How should I use this book? 8

PART I: ZOTERO GENERAL OVERVIEW 11

2: Getting started with Zotero 13
Installing Zotero 13
The Zotero workspace 14
Choosing your preferences 16
Setting up your free Zotero account 17
Retrieving sample data for *Zotero for Genealogy* 19
Getting help 20
Summary 21

3: Documenting your research 23
Choosing your citation style 23
Viewing the Research List 24
Creating a research citation 25
Quick data entry options 30
Adding notes 32
Deleting and restoring research items 34

Adjusting panes and font sizes....................34
Creating tags....................37
Identifying related records....................38
Summary....................39

4: Organizing research collections 41

Using Zotero collections....................42
Research records inside collection folders....................44
Moving subcollections....................46
Deleting collections and subcollections....................46
Summary....................47

5: Managing your attachments....................49

Before you start attaching....................50
Creating file attachments....................53
Restoring broken attachment links....................57
Summary....................58

6: Searching, sorting and finding your research....................59

Basic sorting....................59
Choosing and controlling columns....................60
Basic searching....................61
Advanced searching....................62
Tags....................66
Summary....................66

PART II: ZOTERO ADD-ONS....................67

7: Zotero Connectors & instant data entry....................69

Installing Zotero Connector....................69
Using the Zotero Connector....................70
Summary....................72

8: ZotFile & advanced PDF management....................73

Installing ZotFile....................73
Creating a ZotFile reading stack....................74
Extracting annotations from PDFs....................77
Summary....................79

9: Word processing & painless citations....................81

Installing the word processing add-on....................81

Zotero tools in your word processor 83
Creating citations in your document 85
Adding multiple Zotero citations 86
Editing a citation 87
Creating a bibliography 89
Summary 90

PART III: APPLYING ZOTERO TO GENEALOGY 93

10: Organizing your filing system 95
The main thing: one system for all 95
My very simple filing system 96
Summary 99

11: One source record or many: a choice 101
A source record with many notes 101
A case study 104
Testing your bibliographic data—Style Preview 105
Summary 106

12: Working with Evidence Explained 107
Evidence Explained and the mission of citations 107
Zotero and *EE* in cooperation 108
Maximizing *EE*-to-Zotero conversions 110
Using what Zotero offers 111
Working around the challenges 113
Handling derivatives 117
Summary 120

13: Research logs & to-do lists 121
Research logs 121
To-do lists 123
Summary 127

14: More of Zotero for Genealogy 129
Zotero on the road 129
Edit in a separate window 130
Collaborating and sharing 131
Other bibliographic software—imports and exports 133
Wrapping up 133

Index......134
About the Author......139

Acknowledgments

I do not recall the first person who told me I should take a look at the Zotero software. Nor the second or third. I am grateful to all who sounded the call until I actually looked beneath the hood and saw the power it offered.

I am grateful to the Corporation for Digital Scholarship and the Roy Rosenzweig Center for History and New Media at George Mason University for creating this gem. And I thank the Andrew W. Mellon Foundation, the Institute of Museum and Library Services, the Alfred P. Sloan Foundation, and every other organization or individual who has funded this work and kept Zotero free. I thank Zotero forum superheroes Dan Stillman and Adam Smith, the "first responders" to essential forum questions over the years.

I thank Dr. Elizabeth Shown Mills for her always immediate, gracious, and sage counsel on this and other things. Her role in the professionalization of genealogy inspires me and fills me with gratitude. She models the excellence we Golden Egg Genealogists™ aspire to.

I thank Emily Richardson, my classmate at the Institute for Genealogy and Historical Research, who first made me think about the dilemma we genealogists face. Who will *want* to inherit forty boxes and four four-drawer filing cabinets filled with a lifetime of research *on paper*? It is for the Emilys of our world I write this guide.

Thank you, Blake Rochester, Linda Balderson, and the members of the Tuscaloosa Genealogical Society for being readers and guinea pigs as I moved past being a user to being a teacher.

Finally, as always, thank you, Mac, for putting up with my disappearance into my laptop every night as I got this project done. And to my fur-babies, Bootz and Skitz, thank you for tiptoeing across the keyboard whenever I needed to remember I have other priorities.

PREFACE

zotero

Zotero revolutionized graduate school for me. It minimized the pain and hassle of gathering years of research, organizing it, analyzing it, and formatting it for publication. It truly harnessed the power of my research.

After graduate school for a doctorate in history, I turned my passion and attention back to my first love: genealogy. At first, I tried the research and documentation methods lauded in one genealogy book or website after another. Each seemed too clunky, too much duplication of effort, too limited, not powerful enough, not secure enough—too much or too little of the things I most needed. Then it suddenly hit me: Zotero, my graduate school miracle, would give me everything I really needed and a whole lot more I wanted for genealogy.

This product is fabulous now for all the reasons it was then, and so many more, when applied to genealogy. Here is just a brief sampling of what Zotero offers genealogists:

- Eliminates paper and physical filing, replacing every file cabinet, box, and paper stack you used to think you had to have.
- Eliminates thousands of keystrokes as Zotero creates citations for you with the click of a button.
- Accesses your citations and notes virtually anywhere you have Wi-Fi and a computing device.
- Extracts the comments you have made and the passages you have highlighted in a text-editable PDF, drawing them into Zotero without retyping.

- Finds anything you have stored, with lightning-fast smart searching—even things you stored away years ago and remember only vaguely if at all.
- Replaces the standard genealogy research log with something much better and more powerful.
- Builds a smart to-do list that eliminates repetitive data entry and is there whenever you need it.

Zotero is a workhorse, a powerhouse, a just plain fantastic tool. And here's the best part—the most unbelievable part:

It's FREE.*

You have nothing to lose in giving this a try. You are about to have control over your genealogical research at last. Read on.

* There is always a footnote when someone says, "It's free," isn't there? Zotero is worth a mint at no charge. Once you discover its value, though, I encourage you to consider contributions to the Roy Rosenzweig Center for History and New Media at https://advancement.gmu.edu/ihm02.

INTRODUCTION TO ZOTERO FOR GENEALOGY

1

I have a confession to make. I almost let Zotero pass me by, for the most superficial and counterintuitive of reasons. In the academic community, I kept hearing people say they were using Zotero for their research. I gave it a quick look a couple of times, but I perceived two strikes against it, and my misjudgment now embarrasses me.

First, Zotero is rather plain in appearance. I have to acknowledge that I am drawn to beauty in software—in everything, really. Surely something this plain showed a lack of care about marketing the product—so why should I trust it?

Second, it is free. I have never trusted free when it comes to software. There always comes that moment when you realize what free has cost you. Perhaps you do work of value in the new software, then discover you have to purchase the premium version if you want to save your work or print it. As I tell my genealogy students: "Free is the path to not free." Except, that is, in Zotero.

When I realized why the developers of Zotero have not invested in the superficial things like good looks, it all made sense. They are not trying to sell it. It is a contribution to the world of research, developed by a global community through the Roy Rosenzweig Center for History and New Media at Virginia's George Mason University. This product, used worldwide by scholars in many fields, has the much-coveted vetting and support of a respected university. It is far less likely to suffer the fate of so many products—obsolescence in a rapidly changing computer environment or being bought up, subsumed, or destroyed by a bigger fish.

Without the need to lure buyers with fancy and memory-intensive pretty interfaces, Zotero's creators have put their focus on what matters most to you and me: getting the job done well.

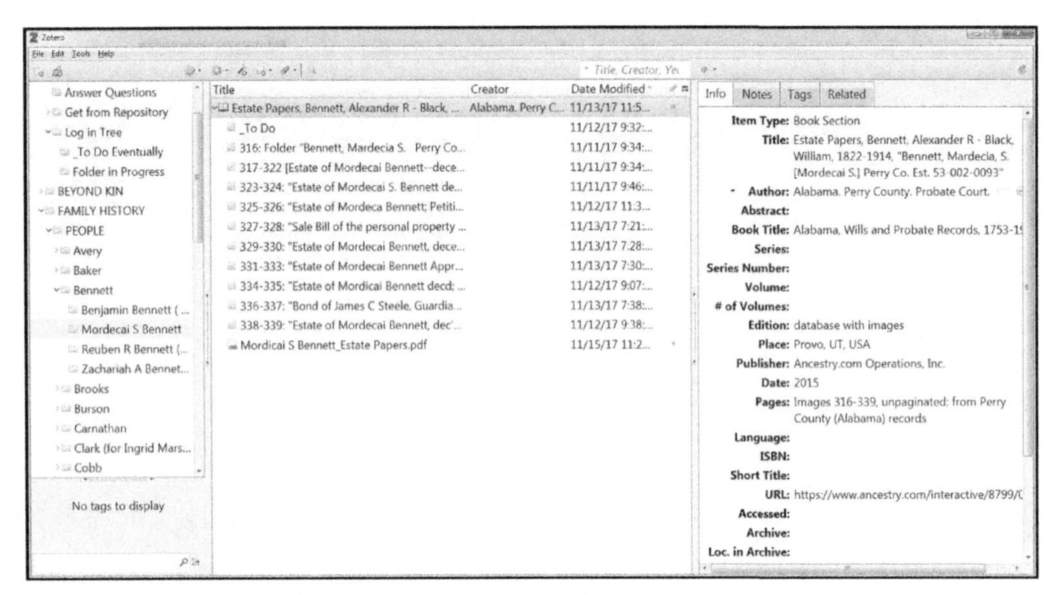

Simple-looking and free, how could it be my answer? I was dubious until it proved so worthy.

WHAT IS ZOTERO?

Zotero's makers describe it in this simple and understated way:

> *Zotero [zoh-TAIR-oh] is a free, easy-to-use tool to help you collect, organize, cite, and share your research sources.*

Zotero offers both structure and flexibility in capturing the information you need to build your family tree, write your family history, work collaboratively with others, research anywhere, and do power genealogy. It blends the structure of controlled databases—encouraging careful citation development—with much of the flexibility you find in notetaking software like Evernote and OneNote.

It presents structured forms for the most-used bibliographic standards of many academic fields, including *The Chicago Manual of Style*, upon which the *Evidence Explained (EE)* citation model—predominant in the field of genealogy—is based. You are able to draw up different sets of fields, depending upon the type of source you are citing. This allows a smart focus on what matters as you are working: eliminating wasted time. While it is not specifically the *EE* model, Chapter 12 describes how to use it to store what you need for the *EE* format.

With Zotero, you can create voluminous notes in plain or formatted text, fully searchable and organized in whatever way suits your filing preferences. You can attach or link to material in numerous forms—documents of various types, spreadsheets, images, videos, audio files, and others.

One of the main powers of Zotero lies in the fact that its makers offer it "open source." In other words, programmers can build on to it, offering extra features. And they have. Wonderful features. Also usually free.

Placing function over form, Zotero offers the environment that can give us real control over data. And doesn't genealogy have SO much information to control? You can truly go paperless, your computer replacing the mountain of paper you might have collected, doing genealogy the old way. This is a new way, a better way, and you will love it.

Upon her mother's death, my friend Emily inherited 40 boxes and four 4-drawer file cabinets of family history research, which she is still sorting years later. (In memory of Dorothy Yoder Coffman)

How does Zotero serve genealogists?

You might be wondering what Zotero gives you that you do not already have in the citation software that comes with Family Tree Maker, RootsMagic, Legacy Family Tree, or whatever tree software you use. The citation tools in family tree software serve to document where you found a particular fact—not to manage the large body of Big-R Research you gather on the way to refining the specific facts that fill in your family story. You might find a record source years before you know that it offers a clue about an as-yet-unidentified ancestor. Zotero holds it in keeping and offers it back up when the time comes. Your family tree software, at least the ones I have seen, are not designed for Big-R Research, but for fact-level citation.

For every genealogical fact you add to your family tree software, you may gather ten, fifty, or a hundred pages of research information. You might research to fill in details about the context of time and place your ancestors inhabited or the legal system or religious culture that surrounded them, affecting the records they kept. Zotero serves the research that allows serious genealogists to truly analyze what they find—to make sense of things more deeply and broadly than the one-fact-at-a-time research that populates the basic family tree.

Before we get to the details, I will answer the question that will soon plague a healthy number of you. You are envisioning the room in your house that is filled with 30 years of collected paper research. How would you even begin to take it online? My counsel is to start by applying what you learn in this book to all new research—everything yet to be done. You can move the older material into Zotero over time if desired. Or you can run a dual paper/online system. Either way, you win.

Zotero serves genealogists in many ways, from storage and retrieval of data to work planning and collaboration. We will examine a number of its functions in-depth in later chapters, but the descriptions below will give you a sense of why this is a tool worth cultivating.

Your research storage and retrieval system

Zotero can replace the file cabinets, binders, boxes, folders, and stacks of unfiled photocopies that the new generations of genealogists dread and avoid. It becomes the map to all of the documents, photos, spreadsheets, and maps you are collecting.

It creates a low-stress, high-yield organizational structure. You do not have to worry so much about putting just the right label on a file folder—afraid you will never find it again. Zotero sports such a great search mechanism that you can find things that would have been lost to you forever in other systems.

Let's say you have a vague recollection that you once found a magazine article from the late 1800s that mentioned your Mayberry family. You do not remember which Mayberry exactly, but there was something about a huge land purchase. You have hundreds of Mayberrys in your tree—thousands of sources that mention them. Your old paper filing system would not make this easy to find. Even if you are using an online notetaking system like OneNote, you could search a very long time. But in Zotero, you can retrieve magazine articles, exclusively—articles you have collected from the late 1800s that mention the name Mayberry. You can tell it to eliminate any that fail to mention land. And you watch the search results reduce down to a manageable few. It works with our faulty memory to make our research findable again.

Even better, you can store more and more without any change in the bulk and weight of your research. You will be amazed at how fast your searches are, even as your records begin to number in the thousands.

Zotero also eliminates an information storage problem peculiar to genealogists. In dealing with family records, a single page might mention 20 people of interest to you. With paper research, you might feel compelled to make 20 copies of the source, filing a copy in each folder for 20 people. If you discover you left a vital piece of citation information out of the original, you have to correct it in 20 places.

With Zotero, on the other hand, you can create just one record and any desirable notes. Then you drag it into an online folder for every person—or every place or every topic—it references. While it then appears everywhere, it only exists once. If you change the record once, you have changed it everywhere.

Your research log

A research log exists to prevent us from repeating work we have already done, to find our way back to work we completed, to remember

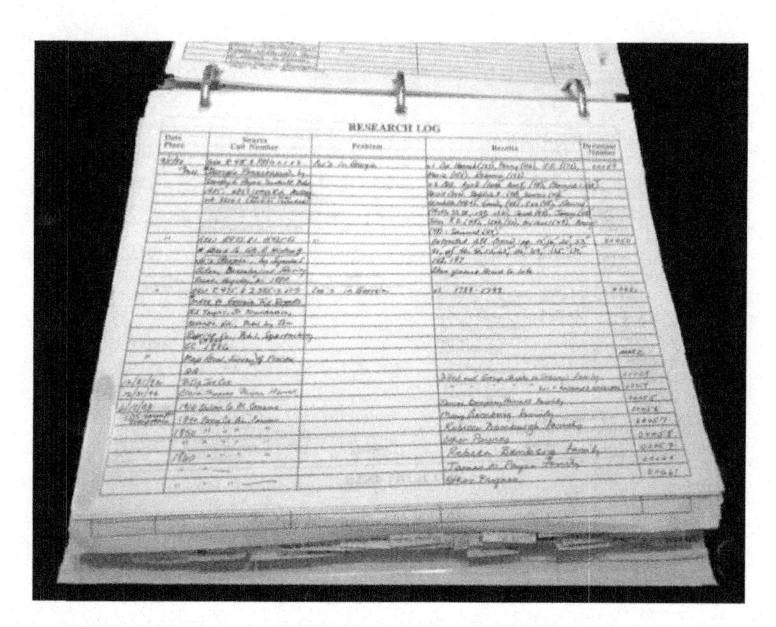

Without Zotero, you might carry a ten-pound paper research log with you to the archives, yet have only a tiny fraction of your information at hand to aid the research. (Courtesy author.)

where we found specific information, to know which surnames we researched in any given record—and often which given name within that grouping. Traditional research logs had a valuable place in genealogical research. But unless you are logging time to a paying client, I see no place for them now—not if you are faithfully using a tool like Zotero. It will capture all you need to know about the source, its citation, location, and collected contents. There is no searching back through old binders to find an earlier reference to a source. You do not have to enter the citation every time you use it. You will store more information, more effectively, with less effort.

Your citation system

While notetaking software like OneNote and Evernote can be very nice for collecting fragments of information, the absence of a systematic structure has drawbacks. Zotero knows what information you are supposed to gather from sources to meet the *Chicago Manual of Style* (*CMOS*) standards or another available style of your choosing. If you tell it you are gathering information from a newspaper, it presents you with the citation data fields you need or want to fill in about the newspaper.

With a free add-on for Microsoft Word, you can turn your Zotero citations into proper *CMOS* footnotes, endnotes, or bibliographical records in articles you write. It essentially puts into your Word environment a window that lets you grab data out of Zotero with a few keystrokes, creating the citations. (An add-on for LibreOffice is also available.)

EE adds some complexity to citation writing, but I will show you how to use the Zotero foundation, building in *EE* information, so that you will have everything you need when you get ready to write for a publication that requires its details.

Your to-do list

Zotero has never marketed itself as to-do software. I happened upon its brilliance for organizing research tasks by accident. I will cover it in more detail in Chapter 13, but the combination of a Zotero add-on that lets you capture bibliographic citations in a single click and Zotero's organizational "collection" structure gives you a real power in planning research trips or tasks.

When a source comes to your attention—something you want to follow up on later—you can create the tickler for yourself, and have a robust roadmap to all of the work you want to do at any given time or in any given place. The most tedious part of research—citation writing—has already been done for you. You simply need to add notes. The information you have gathered then becomes your tickler file for the work needed to follow up after a research trip, processing the information you found.

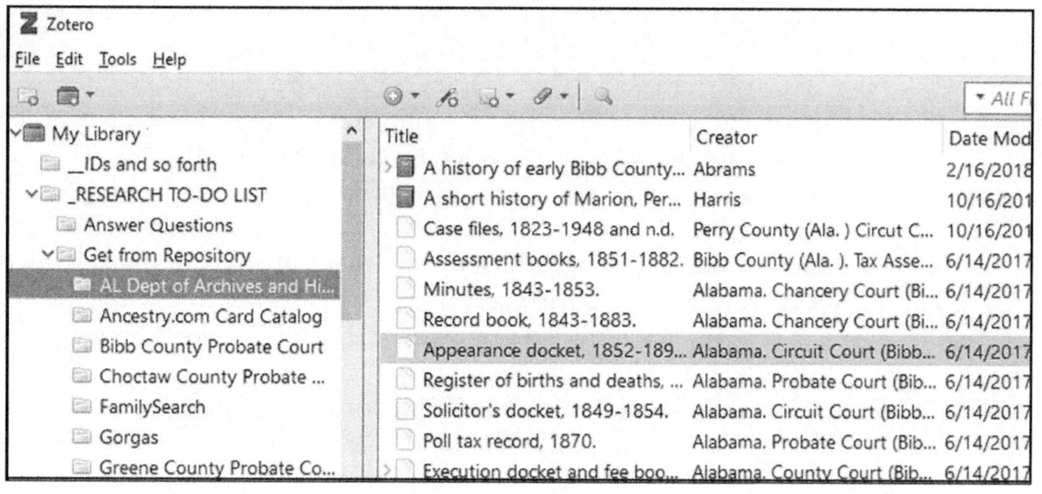

Zotero becomes a robust to-do list for your research trips, preparing you for capturing research notes, and creating your post-research follow-up tickler as you go.

Your collaboration tool with other family researchers

Zotero understands that scholars and researchers are often working in teams. It allows you to share the work you are doing, so everyone in your team can find what has been done. Genealogy works best when researchers share knowledge. Cousins, siblings, or related generations find themselves wanting to collaborate, and you can do it with Zotero. You can create an environment where multiple people are adding to and borrowing from the same set of research notes.

Your portable wonder

We need portability for so many reasons in genealogy. Our research may take us anywhere in the world. In packing, we never know what tidbit of information we will need from our files in order to uncover the next hidden treasure. We never know when an hour will open up on an unrelated trip, allowing us to do unplanned work on our genealogy. And we do not know when it will become our turn to close out this life and pass our research to descendants or relatives. They likely will not welcome a room or even a file cabinet full of files, but hopefully will want your data, well organized, fully online, and portable on a removable hard drive or in the cloud.

How should I use this book?

Many, maybe even most, of you will learn best by reading through this book front to back. It will bring you knowledge in the order you need it. You will learn about things in one chapter that serve you in the next. You might even prefer to read it completely before applying any of it.

Let me confess up front, though, that I have never had the patience to learn so systematically. I want to install the software and start playing with it. I usually come to the book with a specific question in my mind—something I want the software to do. And until I answer that question, nothing else will stick in my nonlinear mind. That will work here, too. Use the Table of Contents or the Index to look for answers to your questions.

For my nonlinear friends, our experimental learning can be powerful in leading us to places the book does not go. But there is also the risk that we will miss something really great in bouncing through the text. So, I encourage you to scan the Table of Contents a few times throughout your self-education, in case there are uses for Zotero that never occurred to you.

In the next chapter, I will show you how to download some sample citations and notes that will be of use as we go through the material in the book. I will also have you creating and changing some of the material in exercises, as we go through. So, again, to the nonlinear ones who want to bounce through, rather than reading front to back, know that you may not be looking at the examples, as intended. At least, download the samples, as instructed.

In the interest of making this book clear and concise, I will be writing about Zotero as I see it, rather than translating the differences for those on other platforms. Know this: Zotero works for Windows, macOS, and Linux. I am on Windows 10, Zotero 5, and I use Microsoft Office 2013 in creating my attachments. You might have to make minor adaptations to instructions if you are a Mac or Linux user or have a different version of Windows or office software. Your workspace might look slightly different. But generally, the instructions should guide you reasonably well through the essential steps.

I must also make some assumptions about you as I decide how to write this guide. I will assume you are familiar with computers sufficiently to install software, to find locations on the Internet, and to know what I mean when I ask you to "click" a button. I also assume you already know a bit about genealogical or historical research. You understand the need for citations. But you do not need to be a power computer user or a power genealogist.

I have divided the book into three parts, to guide us through the process:

Part I	Introduces the basic functions of Zotero, applicable to anyone using the software and not just genealogists.
Part II	Describes several add-on features, external tools that expand Zotero's power in invaluable ways.
Part III	Applies Zotero to the complexities of genealogical research.

So, that is enough about what we are going to do. Let's start *doing* Zotero.

PART I:
ZOTERO GENERAL OVERVIEW

Part I takes readers through the installation, setup, and essential functions of Zotero. It will guide you to a set of materials online that you can download and use to illuminate the examples and exercises in the text. We will not go too deeply here into genealogy-specific questions—giving you the broad overview first. We will talk about genealogical applications in Part III.

GETTING STARTED WITH ZOTERO

2

This chapter will take you through the basics of installing and setting up Zotero, finding your way around its environment, syncing your work, and getting online help.

INSTALLING ZOTERO

Zotero offers a simple and straightforward installation, which will work much like other standard installations on your computer.

Step 1 Go to the Zotero home site at zotero.org.

Step 2 Click the **Download Now** button to find your software download options on the left side of the window.

Step 3 For Windows users, click **Download**. Mac and Linux users may download Zotero by clicking on the appropriate link just below the Windows option.

Step 4 Click on the button in the bottom-left corner of the window, which should display the name of the downloaded file. Or, go to the folder where your computer stores downloaded files and click on the most recent file.

Step 5 Your computer may ask if you will allow the app to make changes to your device. Click **Yes**.

Step 6 From this point forward, follow the installation instructions on your desktop, accepting the options as presented unless you are a power user who understands the effects of alternative choices.

Step 7 Launch Zotero, when the installation is complete.

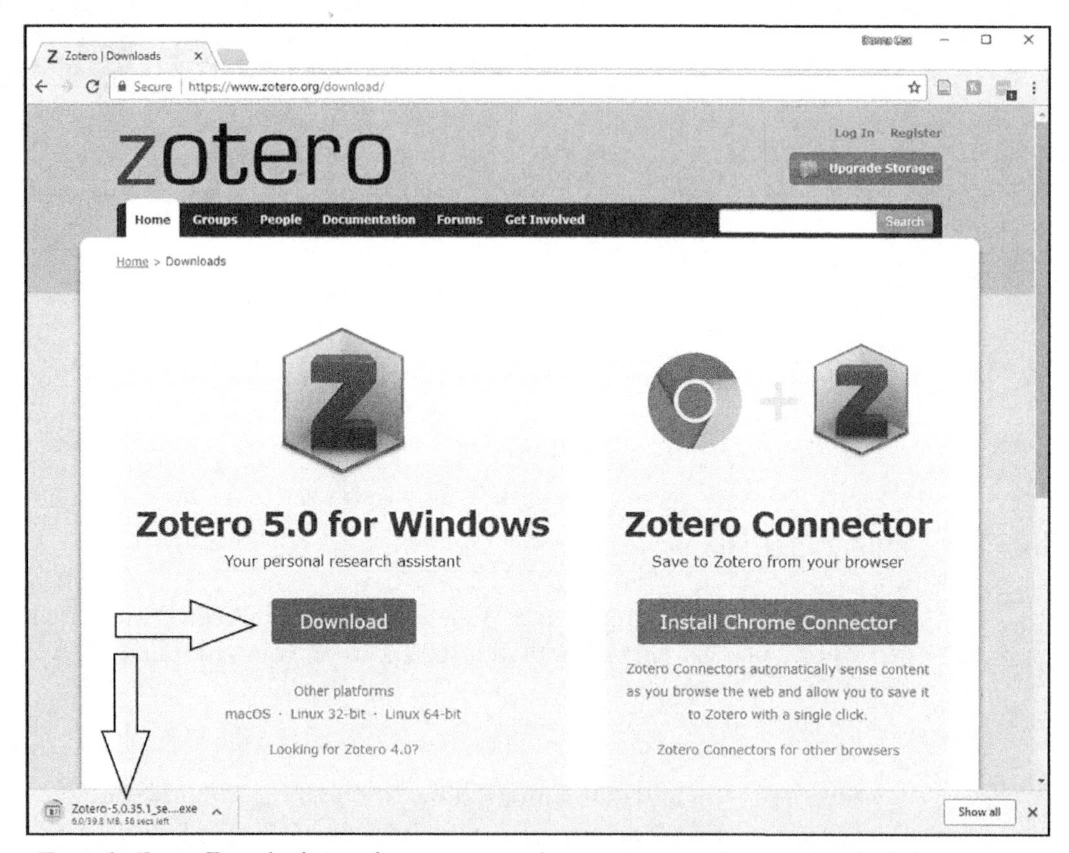

From the Zotero Download view, choose your system's operating environment to download the software to your computer. Click the downloaded file at the bottom left.

THE ZOTERO WORKSPACE

Zotero is designed very simply, with most of its content and features accessible on or within a click of the main workspace. Your Zotero workspace will be nearly empty as we begin, but the illustrations here will show you what it looks like as you populate it with data.

The main desktop window includes four panes, three of which you can remove from sight when it is helpful. Most of your work will be done in these panes, which are interactive—each one being affected by choices made in the others.

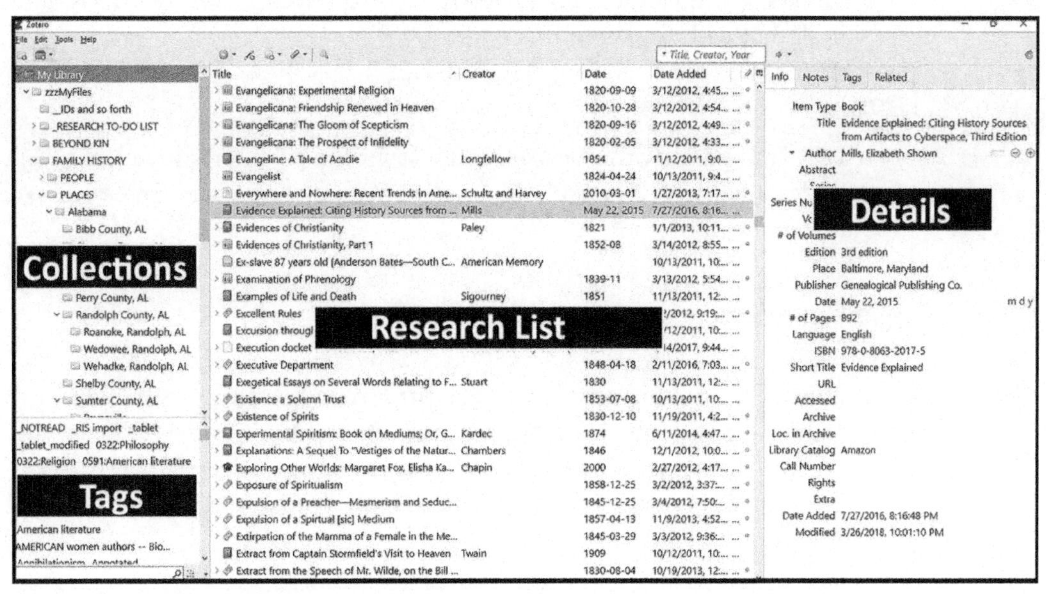

The bulk of your work in Zotero is done in these four interactive panes, displayed here in the default Standard View.

Collections

The Collections pane displays your organizational structure—in essence, the folders to hold your information. You can create multiple layers of subfolders to control your collections further, going far deeper in nested folders than most of us would ever need for our filing.

Research List

We will refer to the center pane as your Research List pane. The research list displayed at any given time depends on what you have selected in the Collections pane. At the top of Collections, you will see *My Library*. When you click on it, the Research List pane displays a master list of every research item you have documented. This allows you to search across all of your records simultaneously or to sort them by various criteria.

Details

The right-most pane has four tabs to allow the gathering of citation information and research notes, the assignment of "tags" or subject headings, and the ability to relate one citation or note to another. When you select a bibliographic citation record in your research list, this pane will show the citation information. If you select a note you have created, that will display in this pane.

Tags

The Tags pane at the bottom left allows you to filter your view to include only those Zotero items assigned a particular tag—in essence, a subject heading.

CHOOSING YOUR PREFERENCES

We will be talking about various preference settings as we get into deeper discussions of features, but let's take a quick glance at the available settings. From the menu, choose **Edit—Preferences**. The toolbar across the top allows you to set preferences in six different categories.

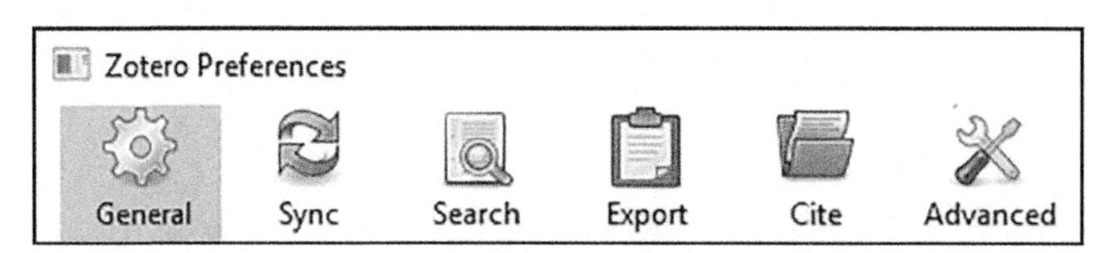

The Preferences toolbar

General	Establishes the preferred workspace view and preferences for the way Zotero will handle materials imported, saved, attached, or copied, among other functions.
Sync	Manages the syncing of your data to Zotero's available cloud storage, including choices about the handling of attachments.
Search	Sets options affecting search speed and the indexing of the contents of embedded PDFs. Primarily for advanced users.
Export	Determines nature and format of information to be exported or copied out of Zotero to other environments. Primarily for advanced users.
Cite	Determines available style standards, inclusion of URLs in citations, modification of styles, and installation of word processing add-ons.

Advanced Sets language options, sets the paths to file storage on the user's personal hard drive, creates keyboard shortcuts, and sets options for advanced users.

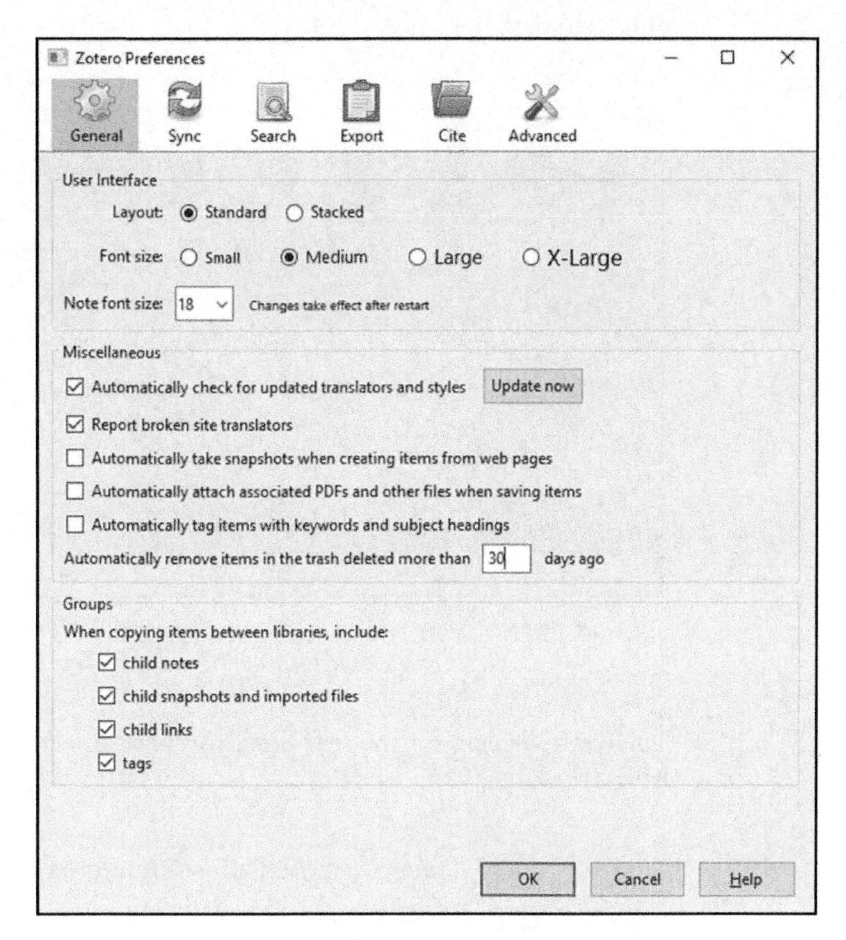

The Preferences view allows you to tailor Zotero for your ideal purposes—everything from its look and feel to its connection to exterior programs and files.

Setting up your free Zotero account

Before we get to the business of adding information to Zotero, let's address the vital need to protect your information. Zotero backs up your data and, if you choose, makes it available for remote access through its cloud sync function.

It offers you 300 MB of free storage for syncing your research. You can make that storage last a very long time by linking rather than embedding attachments (see Chapter 5). But do not worry if you have masses of resource-intensive data you want to embed. Zotero offers unlimited data for a reasonable price.

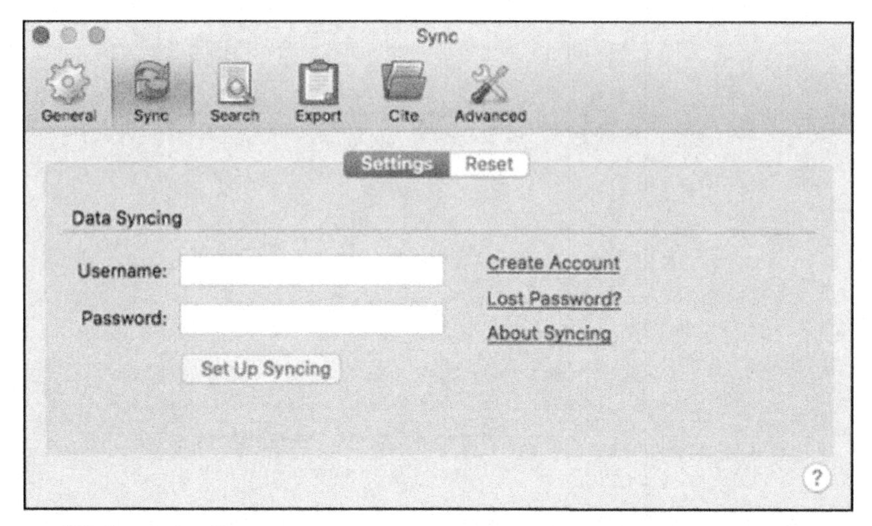

With your free Zotero account, you can sync up to 300 MB of data, with more space available for a very reasonable price.

To sync your data for the first time, you need to establish an account with Zotero.

Step 1	On the Menu, choose **Edit—Preferences**.
Step 2	Click the **Sync** button on the toolbar.
Step 3	Click **Create Account** and follow Zotero's instructions to establish your account.
Step 4	Return to the Data Syncing window, enter the Username and Password set up in Step 3, and click **Set Up Syncing**.
Step 5	Accept the defaults on Zotero's Sync panel for the moment. As we look at the choices related to attachments later, you might want to alter these values.

RETRIEVING SAMPLE DATA FOR *ZOTERO FOR GENEALOGY*

As we go through the various instructions and exercises in the chapters ahead, you will benefit from having a set of practice data, which you can get from the Zotero website. You can do this by joining an online Zotero group, which will open the dataset on your own computer. Follow these instructions:

Step 1 Close your desktop Zotero software.

Step 2 Go to https://www.zotero.org/groups/ in your internet browser.

Step 3 If you are not already logged in, click **Log In** in the top-right corner, and enter your username and password.

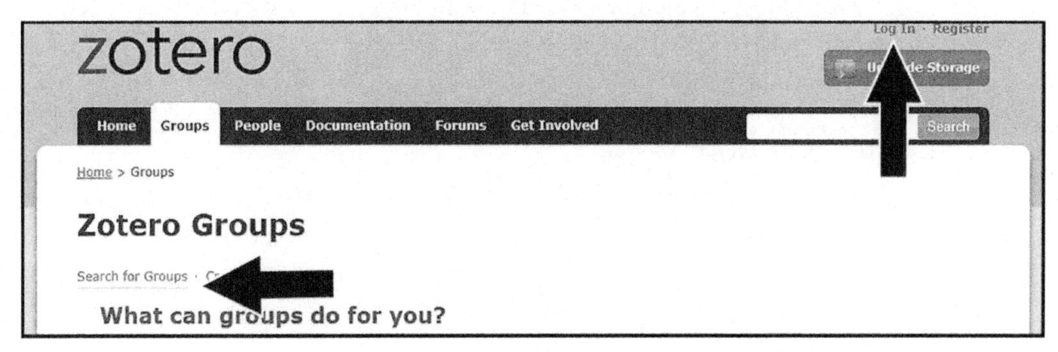

Log in to Zotero's online site and choose to Search for Groups.

Step 4 Click **Search for Groups**, just below the page title.

Step 5 In the search box, type "Baker Genealogy Exercises" and click **Search Groups**.

Step 6 In the search results, click on the title **Baker Genealogy Exercises**.

Step 7 On the right-hand side of the screen, click the **Join** button to obtain access.

Step 8 Close Zotero.org and reopen your desktop software.

Step 9 In the Collections pane, look toward the bottom for *Group Libraries*. Beneath it, you should now see a gold folder called *Baker Genealogy Exercises*. Nested under this, you

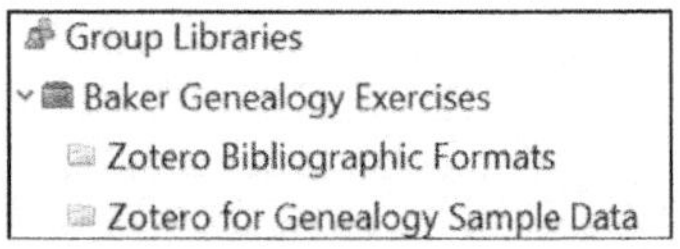

Group Libraries
Baker Genealogy Exercises
Zotero Bibliographic Formats
Zotero for Genealogy Sample Data

should see two yellow folders titled *Zotero Bibliographic Formats* and *Zotero for Genealogy Sample Data.* (If you do not see them, click on the arrow to the left of the gold folder to expand the contents.) Drag and drop the subfolders on top of *My Library*, which is at the top of the Collections pane. The folders will now be copied to the new location—appearing in both places. We will work in the copies in *My Library*, for our exercises.

GETTING HELP

Zotero offers several avenues to assistance, as you master this phenomenal tool. While Zotero has no support hotline, its documentation, troubleshooting guidelines, and forums have assisted me very well for everything I have ever needed. You also have a mechanism to report errors to the programming staff. All of these help features can be accessed through the Help menu.

Documentation

Zotero covers the essentials in its online documentation. It will be a nice complement to this book, which does not claim or attempt to cover every detail of setting up and using the software.

Troubleshooting information

Zotero's online troubleshooting page guides you through the steps you need to follow before escalating a perceived problem. It will ensure you are on the most up-to-date version of the software. It will offer you a report of all known issues with the software. And it offers Frequently Asked Questions to cover the typical issues.

Forums

I have found the forums to be remarkably helpful in getting resolutions to issues. Zotero staff and power users typically monitor the forums and usually respond very quickly. I do not recall ever posting a question that was not speedily and effectively answered. You will need your Zotero login to post a message to the board.

Report errors

If the Zotero software generates an error, you can choose the Report Errors option from the Help menu, follow the prompts, and send the error to Zotero for investigation.

Updating your Zotero software

Zotero will routinely check for the availability of a newer version of the software. Or you may force it to check by clicking "Check for Updates" on the Help menu.

SUMMARY

By now, you should have Zotero installed and a Zotero account set up online. You should have sample data in your desktop for use in the exercises we will do throughout the book. We are ready to get to the details of entering basic research.

Documenting Your Research

3

Zotero offers flexibility and shortcuts in citing research and gathering notes. We will start with the basics here, adding more layers of usefulness as we get into the discussions of add-ons and the genealogical applications for Zotero in later chapters.

Choosing Your Citation Style

Zotero will guide you in recording your research based on the style you wish to use in citing your sources, should you decide to publish your research. Zotero supports numerous different citation styles, and the number keeps growing to support the needs of various scholarly fields and publishing environments. Most genealogists will find the *Chicago Manual of Style* (*CMOS*) format the preferred template.

It is possible to shift from one style to another, though some data may be lost in the transfer. To set the style you prefer to use, select **Edit—Preferences** and choose **Cite** from the toolbar. For our work here, select

The Chicago Manual of Style 17th edition (full note)[*]

Select the box to **Include URLs of paper articles in references**. (You may later choose to deselect this if you do not want the lengthy URL addresses in your citations.) Then, click **OK** to return to the main window.

---

[*] *CMOS* is in its 17th edition as of this printing. If a later version is available by the time you read this, choose that.

VIEWING THE RESEARCH LIST

Let's take a look at items in your Research List, so you can get familiar with how Zotero structures and displays them. In the Collections pane to the left, click on your new folder under *My Library*, the folder called *Zotero for Genealogy Sample Data*. A set of records will appear in the Research List pane.

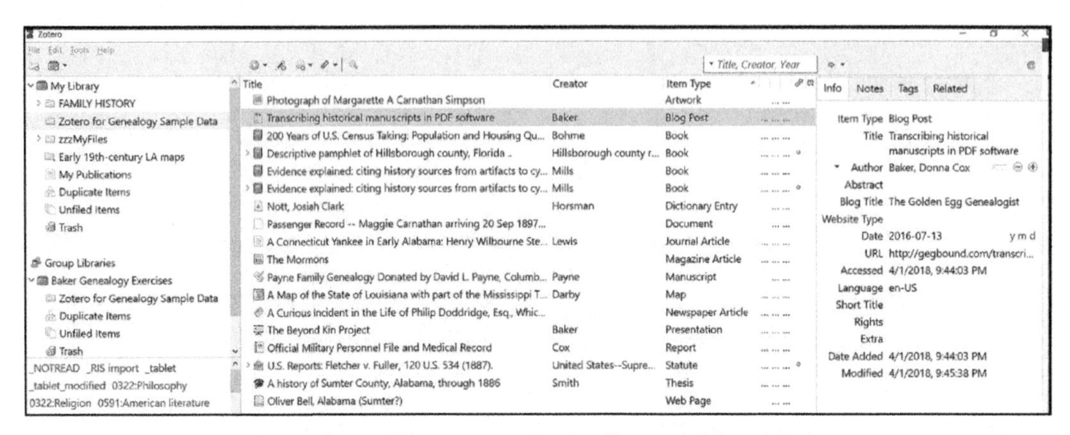

A sample set of data appears in your Research List when you select the sample folder you copied into My Library.

You will notice to the left of each source citation appearing in your Research List one of a varied set of icons representing the type of source. Next to books, you will see the image of a book, a document icon beside a document, a graduation cap beside a dissertation, and so on.

One of the great powers of Zotero lies in its ability to guide you to the information you might need to gather for all of the different types of citations. It bases its guidance on the citation style you selected in "Choosing your citation style" above.

Click on your sample research list items one by one. Notice what appears to the right in your Details pane. The Item Type at the top of the Details pane shows you what type of citation you are viewing. Zotero displays beneath that the set of fields you will want to consider completing for that item type.

Creating a Research Citation

You enter a new bibliographic citation by clicking on the **New Item** button on the toolbar above the Research List. In the menu it displays, you choose the **Item Type**. Depending upon the type you choose, the Info tab will display a targeted set of fields. The illustrations below shows a "Book" type on the left and a "Report" type on the right. While some fields are shared between them, others like the book's ISBN or the report's institution are not.

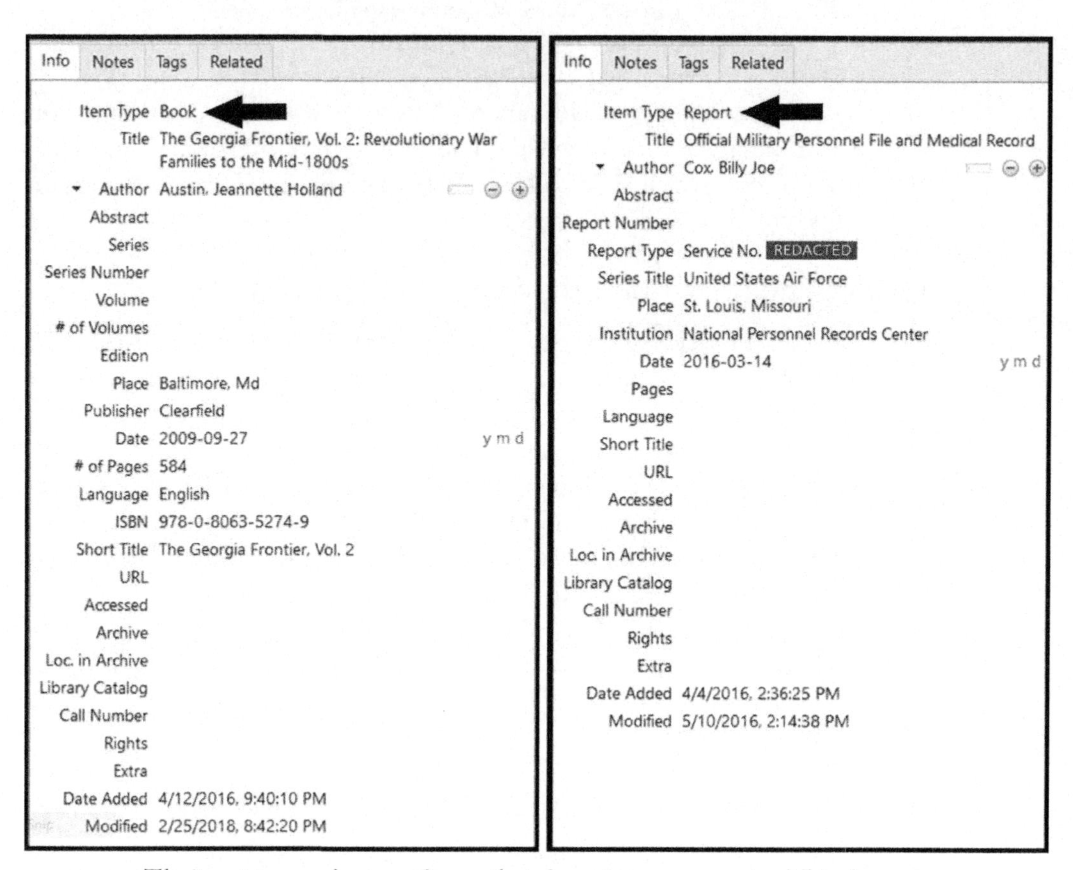

The item type you choose configures the information you may enter. This shows two different views of the Details pane, one a book and the other a report.

Some fields will not be included in actual bibliographic citations drawn from the data collected here. The dates added and modified, for example, are in the Details pane and useful for your reference. They are not of value in the bibliographic citation you might draw from this for use in an article or book you are writing. In *CMOS* style, the book citation data above is formatted this way:

Austin, Jeannette Holland. *The Georgia Frontier*, Vol. 2: Revolutionary War Families to the Mid-1800s. Baltimore, MD: Clearfield, 2009.

The military personnel record, cited with the Report item type yields this citation, in *CMOS* format:

Cox, Billy Joe. "Official Military Personnel File and Medical Record." Service No. [redacted]. United States Air Force. St. Louis, Missouri: National Personnel Records Center, March 14, 2016.

As you begin to build data in Zotero, it will attempt to save you keystrokes in several data fields. The author, publisher, and place fields, among others, will start to type ahead for you, inserting possible options already used in the system.

Authors, editors, and other key contributors

Most of the fields are self-explanatory, but the author, date, and URL fields have special features. The small arrow to the left of the Author field allows you to change the role of the contributors to the record source you are documenting.

This menu also allows you to rearrange the order of multiple contributors. This will affect their display in your formal citations. The **plus** and **minus** buttons to the right of the names allow you to add or remove contributors. In this example, you have co-editors Jones and Gandrud.

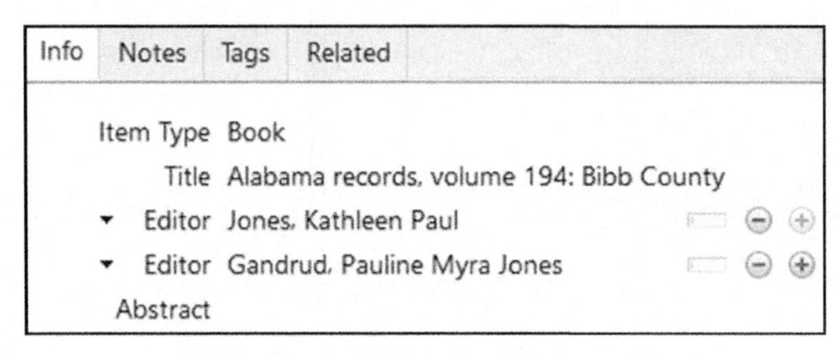

Zotero allows multiple authors, editors, or other participants in the creation of the source record.

The available creator roles change, depending upon the type of citation. If you are capturing the citation information for the Book item type, your options are Author, Contributor, Editor, Series Editor, or

Translator. If you use the Book Section item type, you are offered both an Author and a Book Author option, which allows you to make note of a book section authored by someone other than the book's main authors or editors.

Zotero takes the roles you choose for creators in the various item types and creates the proper *CMOS* format for that type of citation. If you are capturing an Interview item type, for example, Zotero will offer you the creator roles of Interview With, Contributor, Interviewer, and Translator. The Interview With person will become the key creator, and Zotero will insert "interview by" and the Interviewer's name—as the style recommends. An interview with Michelle Obama by Oprah Winfrey on NBC News might look like this:

> Obama, Michelle. Interview on "Becoming" book. Interview by Oprah Winfrey. Television. November 14, 2018. NBC News Online. https://www.nbcnews.com/video/oprah-interviews-former-first-lady-michelle-obama-1370056771738

If you are recording a Letter item type, you will need to designate both an Author and a Recipient. Zotero will take these two roles and create the proper citation format of [Author] to [Recipient]. In the section titled "Testing your bibliographic data—Style Preview" in Chapter 11, I will demonstrate how to preview the citations Zotero will create. You will want to experiment in the use of this creator field to optimize your citations.

Date formats

You may enter a date in any of a number of standard formats, and Zotero will interpret it, as needed. The letters to the right of the date reveal the interpretation Zotero has made. In the first case below, the date was entered in a year-month-day (y m d) arrangement. The second was formatted with date-month-year (d m y). While these dates would sort badly in alphanumeric order, Zotero knows how to convert the dates behind the scenes, sorting them properly.

Date	1858-04-17	y m d
Date	16 December 1823	d m y

Use the date format you prefer, and Zotero will interpret it.

In the image below, you see the Research List of your sample data sorted in date order, despite the various date formats used.

Title	Creator	Date
A Map of the State of Louisiana with part of th...	Darby	1816
A Curious Incident in the Life of Philip Doddri...		1844-03-16
The Mormons		March 1851
A history of Sumter County, Alabama, through...	Smith	1988
200 Years of U.S. Census Taking: Population a...	Bohme	1989
A Connecticut Yankee in Early Alabama: Henry...	Lewis	2006-04
Official Military Personnel File and Medical Re...	Cox	3/14/2016
Transcribing historical manuscripts in PDF soft...	Baker	2016-07-13
The Beyond Kin Project	Baker	9 Feb 2018

Zotero supports multiple date formats, allowing for proper sorting.

While Zotero will allow you to type text or date ranges into the date field, it cannot include them in a citation. It will assume that the last episode of four digits that appears anywhere in the date field is the year. It will treat it as a year in the citation. You may get creative with data entry in many Zotero fields, but this one needs to be a specific day, month, or year.

The hidden URL button

For a convenient but obscure feature of Zotero, click on the label **URL** beside a web address in a citation. Zotero will open a browser to the stored web address.

URL http://stlcourtrec ords.wustl.edu/index.php
Accessed 9/4/2017

*Click **URL** to go to the stored web address.*

Exercise 1: Add a book

Let's walk through the creation of a research citation record for a published book. We will choose one that most of us know well: Elizabeth Shown Mills's *Evidence Explained: Citing History Sources from Artifacts to Cyberspace.*

Step 1 Click the **New Item** button on your toolbar and select **Book** from the drop-down list. If it does not appear, click **More** and choose it from the submenu.

You will then see the "Book" item type in the top of the Details pane display.

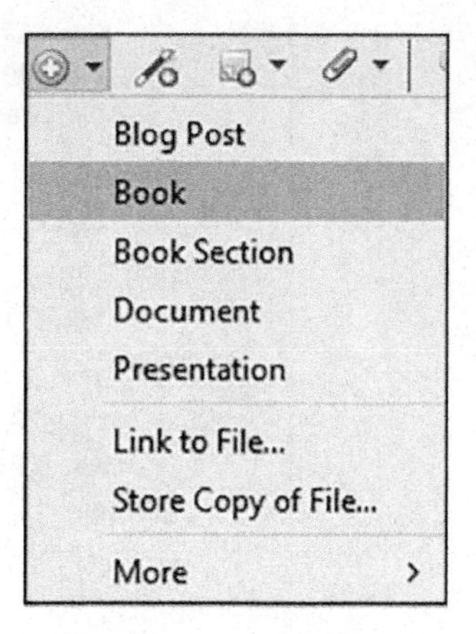

The New Item button in the top-left corner of the Research List toolbar brings up a menu of item types.

Step 2 Type in the Title: "Evidence explained: citing history sources from artifacts to cyberspace." Tab to the next field.

Step 3 Enter "Mills" in the Author (last) field, tab over, and type "Elizabeth Shown" in the **Author** (first) field.

Step 4 Move down and type "3" in the Edition field; "Baltimore, Maryland" in Place; "Genealogical Publishing Co." in Publisher; and "2017" in Date. Tab out of the field to save the data.

Zotero will save data each time you exit a field. It has added the **Date Added** and **Modified** fields for your reference. The first date will not change, always letting you know when you first consulted this source. The second will always let you know the last time you did. If you want to keep a complete record of every time you consulted the source, you can use the notes feature to capture anything of value.

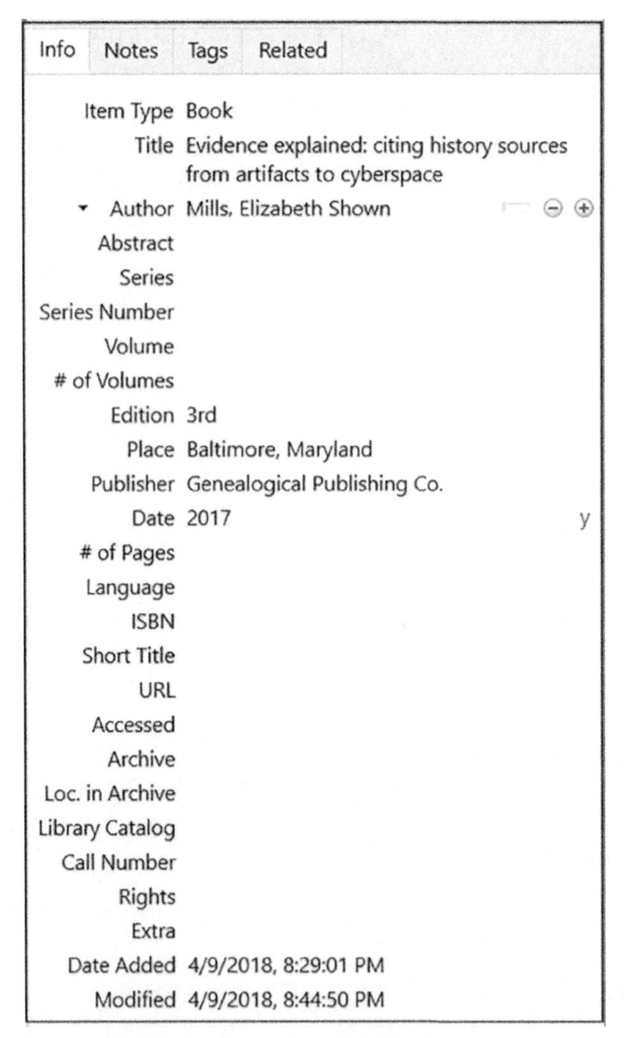

You choose how much or little information to gather on a citation.

Quick Data Entry Options

Add item(s) by identifier

Zotero allows you to automate data entry if you have standard identifiers for your sources. On the main workspace toolbar, the **Add Item(s) by Identifier** button allows you to take this shortcut. If you enter a book's International Standard Book Number (ISBN), a digital resource's Digital Object Identifier (DOI), or a

PubMed Identifier (PMID) for publications in the life sciences, Zotero will pull information into a new citation item for you.

The accuracy of the data pulled in this way depends on the diligence of the person who entered the bibliographic citation into the external databases Zotero consults. You will want to verify that the information came through properly, and make any needed corrections.

Exercise 2: Add book using ISBN

Step 1 Type the following ISBN into the field to have Zotero pull in *Evidence Explained* again: **9780806320403**

Step 2 Press **Enter.** That's it! You have added the book.

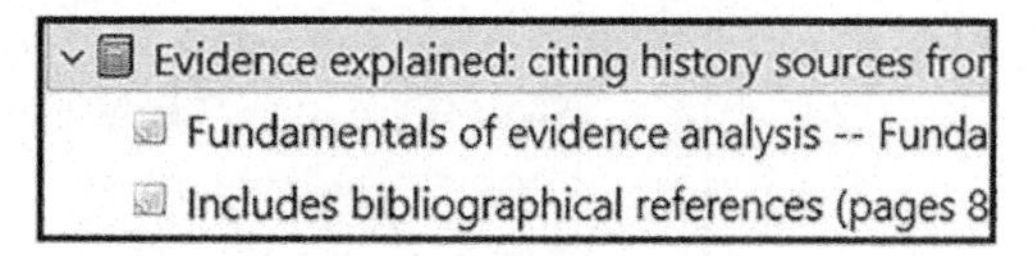

An imported citation brings metadata with it.

You should now have two copies of the Mills book in your Research List. Click on each one to view the data pulled into your Details pane. Assuming nothing has changed in the world's library information or "metadata" since the writing of this book, you will notice that this method pulled in more information than we typed in the manual record. Even better, it will have attached to the citation some notes that describe the book. To see the notes, look for an arrow (>) to the left of the record in the Research List. Click on the arrow and expand what is beneath. The notes have a sticky note icon to the left. When you click on the note title in the Research List, the notes appear in the Details pane. This tool can save you much typing and usually some typographical errors.

Sneak preview of the Zotero Connector

If you are adding a citation record to Zotero from a book in your hand, the option above works great. However, I find myself much more often grabbing source information from online tools, like WorldCat.org, a local library's online catalog, or even Amazon. In Part II, I will introduce you to the feature that first sold me on Zotero as my must-have tool for graduate school. The Zotero Connector allows you to create a robust Zotero citation record with only one click. Stay tuned for that.

Adding Notes

You can create as many notes as you want for any given research citation. As you do, a list will begin to form in the Notes tab in the Details pane. To create a new note on an existing citation, click **Add**.

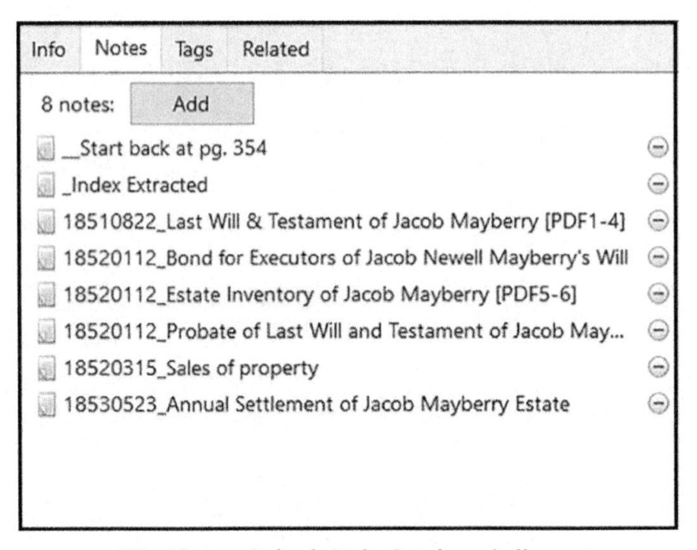

The Notes tab displays the first line of all notes associated with the selected source.

You can create notes that stand alone in your Research List. These can be pieces of information unconnected to a citation but useful to you—say, the address and operating hours of a particular archive.

As you type a new note, the first line you type will be treated as the note's title. You can find and replace text within a note by using the binoculars on the toolbar. Notes text can be plain or rich-text (formatted) and can interpret and display text formatted by HTML coding.

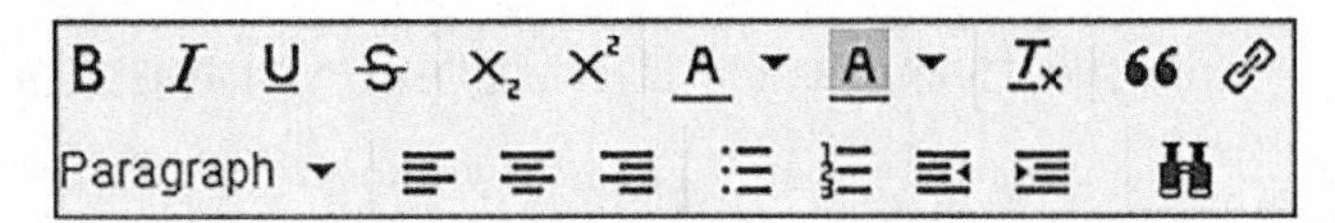

Zotero's rich-text notes can be formatted with tools on the toolbar. The binoculars allow searching within the text.

Zotero offers basic "rich text" formatting tools, allowing you to bold, italicize, underline, strikethrough, superscript, subscript, color, or highlight text. You can create block quotes, hyperlinks, paragraph styles, varied alignments, bullets, numbering, and indentations. It does not support the assignment of fonts besides those of the designated styles, but rich text in a wide range of fonts can be pasted in from other software tools, like Microsoft Word.

Basic text serves well for most notetaking in Zotero, but if you need special formatting, such as tables, you can also create the content in software such as Microsoft Word, and paste it into the note.

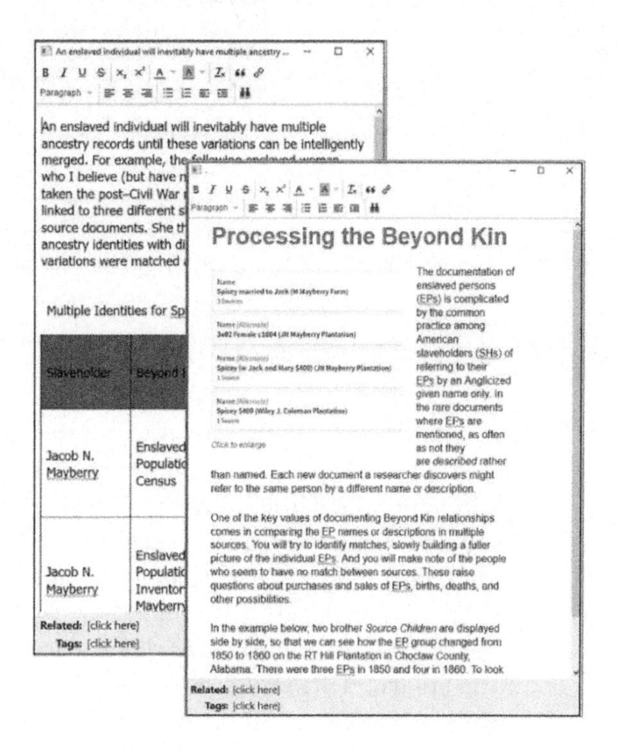

Complex formatting can be pasted into Zotero from browsers or other software, like Microsoft Word.

The **Edit in a separate window** option that appears at the bottom of the Notes pane allows you to pop the pane out of the larger workspace. This can become very helpful when you are taking notes from another window on your computer. You are able to narrow the note window beside the window from which you are extracting information. In Chapter 14, I will describe how to apply this to genealogical transcription projects.

DELETING AND RESTORING RESEARCH ITEMS

If you desire to delete a research item completely from your Zotero data, click on *My Library* in your Collections pane to reveal your entire library. Find the item, right-click on it, and choose **Move Item to Trash**. The item will no longer appear in *My Library* but will remain available in Zotero's trash bin, until you choose to empty it.

Zotero's Trash holds deleted items awaiting your final choice to empty them permanently.

Zotero's *Trash* can be found toward the bottom of the *My Library* (upper) section of your Collections pane. When you click on it, all of the records slated for removal will appear in your Research List. If the item deleted was one of multiple attachments and notes beneath a single citation, the whole citation set will appear. Only the one to be deleted will appear in regular text format. All of the other items in that group, including the main citation, will be dimmed out and are not at risk of being deleted.

If you want to recover one of the trash items back to active use in your library, right-click on the specific item and choose **Restore to Library**. The item will be available again for use. If you want to permanently delete one of the items, without emptying the entire trash bin, right-click on the item and click **Delete Item**. To empty the trash completely, right-click on the Trash collection in the Collections pane and click **Empty Trash**.

Keep in mind that the data in your trash bin counts against the storage limits you have in the Zotero cloud. You will want to empty the trash on a regular basis to free up cloud space.

ADJUSTING PANES AND FONT SIZES

You can adjust the visual appearance of Zotero to optimize the workspace for your particular needs. Go to the User Interface section of your Zotero Preferences—General tab to alter your workspace view. You may find that various tasks you are performing are optimized by changing these settings. You can change them as often as you like.

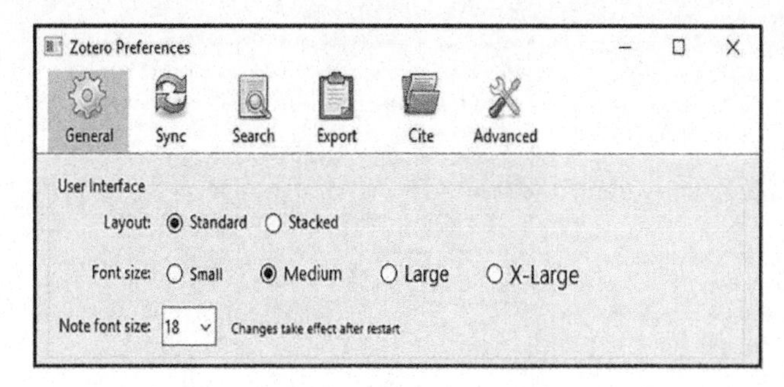

The preferences above yield the altered workspace view (next page).

Zotero Preferences—User Interface

Layout
The Standard view places the Research List and Details panes side by side. The Stacked view places the list above details, with both panes at a maximized width. You may choose to change the layout from time to time, depending on the task at hand.

Font size
Four font size options allow you to decide how much information you can see at a time—and how easy it is to see. If you choose a small font, you will see more data—a larger font shows less at a time but is easier to see. This affects all fonts except those in your notes field.

Note font size
Within any given note, you have substantial control over your font size. Choose an option in the drop-down list or type your own size over the default. The example below shows the notes font set at a very large size, which can be very helpful for those with vision challenges. At the present time, Zotero requires you to close and reopen the program to activate a change in font size for the notes.

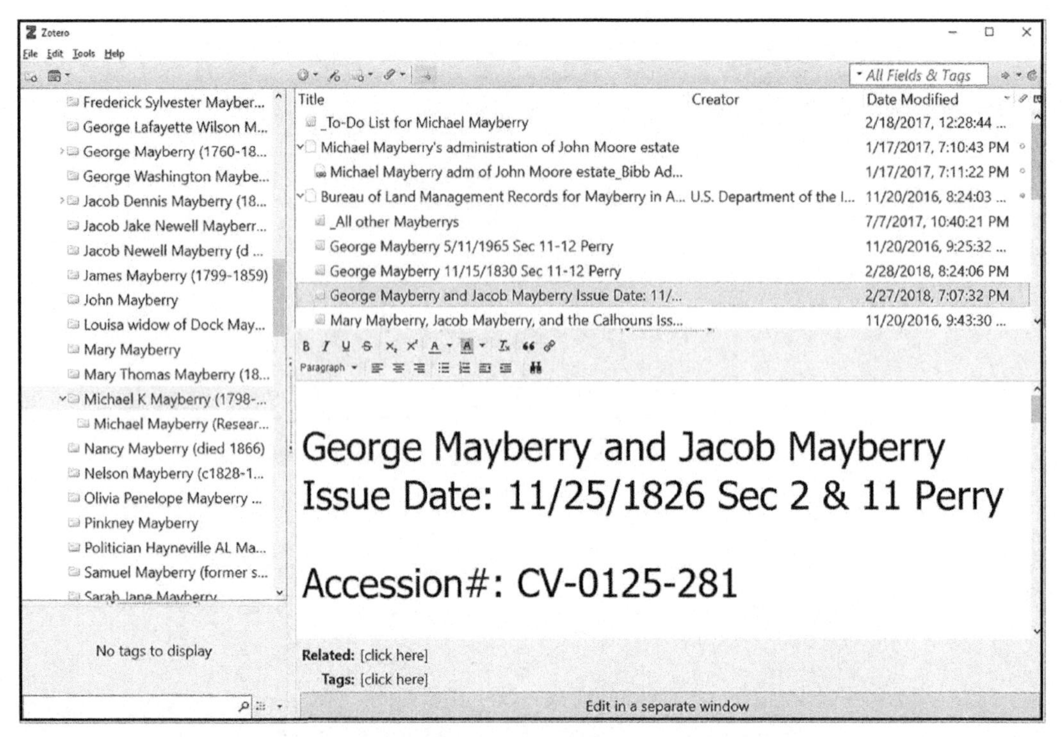

This workspace view now "stacks" the Research List and Details panes on top of each other, rather than side by side. It displays the main font as X-large, the Notes font sized at 48.

Adjusting panes

The size (or even presence) of the workspace panes can also be adjusted, allowing you to determine what data you will see more of and what you will see less of. When you let your cursor rest on top of the dividing line between panes, you will see a two-way arrow appear. Click and drag it in the direction you would like to move the dividing line.

You can drag a divider all the way to the left or right edge of the workspace to make an entire pane or set of panes disappear. You can then drag that outer border again to make the pane reappear.

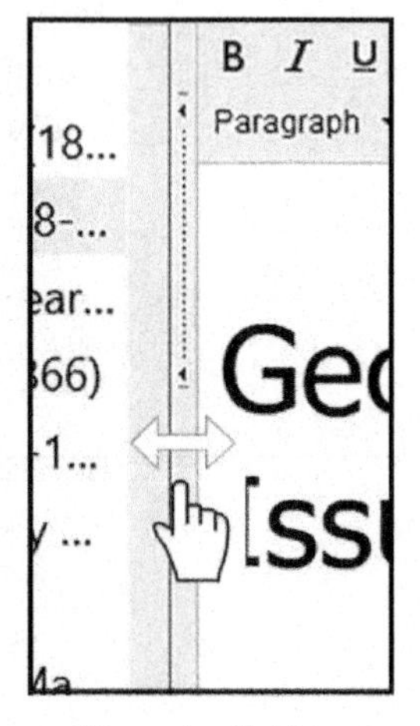

Drag the divider to alter panes.

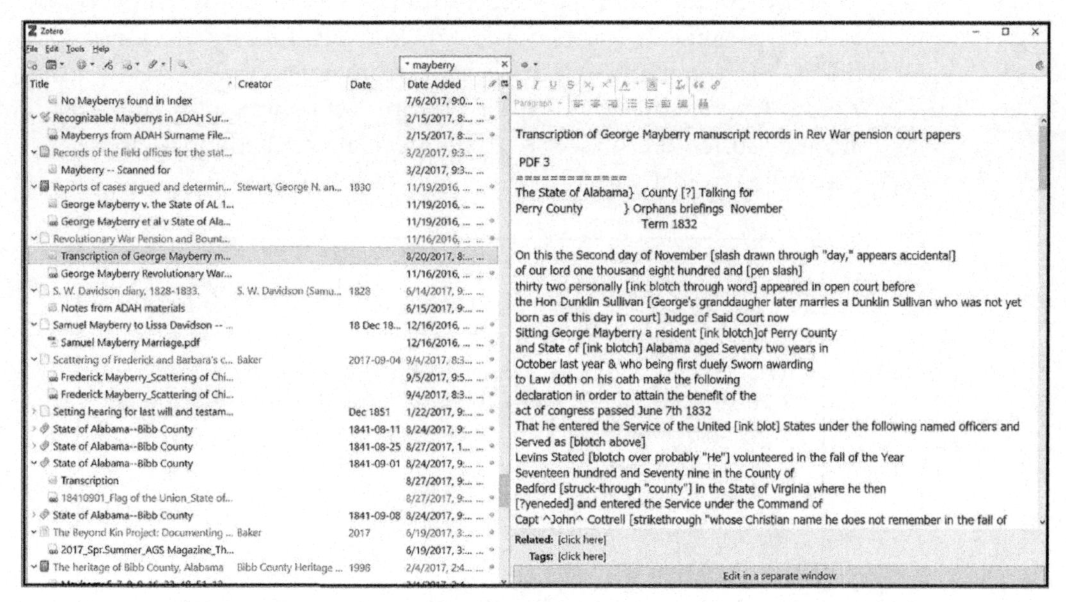

By dragging the divider between the Collections and Research List panes toward the left, the Collections and Tags panes have disappeared, making more room for the Research List and Details.

CREATING TAGS

In Zotero, "tags" are essentially subject headings—words that connect a group of your research items together under common themes. You may assign any tag that is of use to you. Click on the **Tags** tab above the citation pane, and choose to **Add**. Once you have created a tag for use on a research item, it will become available from a drop-down list, any time you want to add it to another research item.

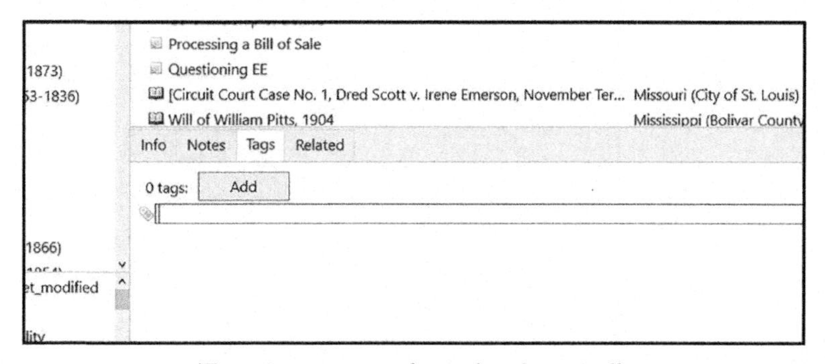

Tags tie your research together thematically.

I use the Tag feature to create for myself an inventory of the books I own. I assign each of them the tag "Personal Library of Donna Cox Baker." As you import research items from external repositories using Zotero Connector (see Chapter 7), some will come with tags already created—often the subject heading metadata created by libraries. You may assign as many to a research item as you like.

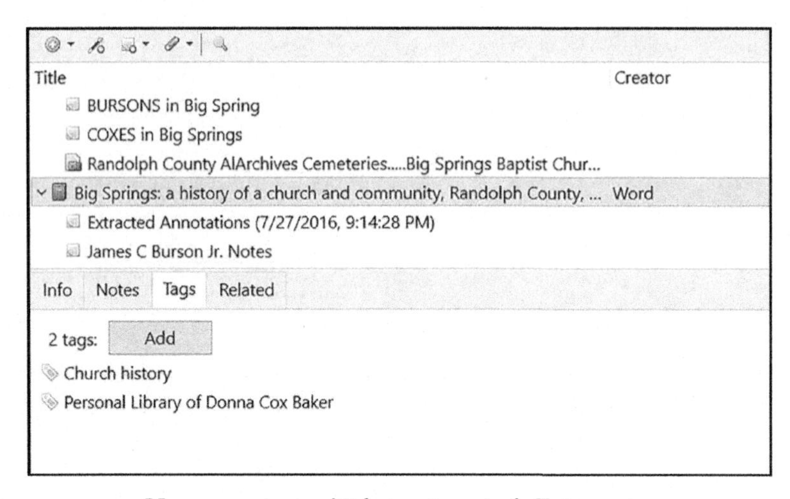

You can assign multiple tags to a single Zotero entry.

IDENTIFYING RELATED RECORDS

The Related records tab allows you to connect specific source records that you want to recall together. For example, you might relate books in a series or a book and all the book reviews you have collected about

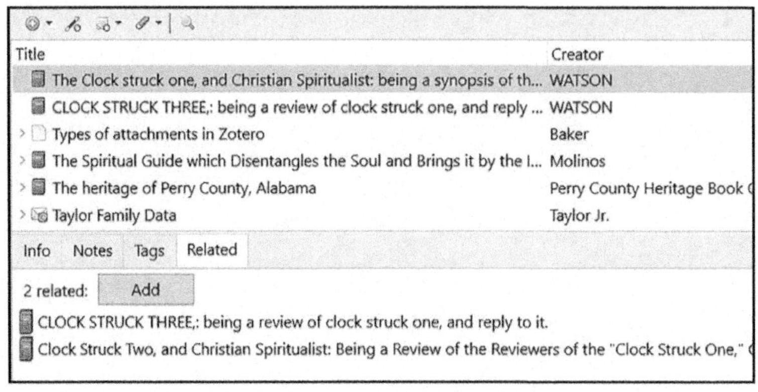

You can create relationships between sources that have a meaning in connection with each other by adding items in the Related tab.

it. Genealogists, of course, have many reasons to connect records together—creating family connections or tying an original courthouse name to the modern name. You add related records in the same way you add tags and notes.

SUMMARY

The creation of research records and notes forms the core function of Zotero, as a data storage tool. The citation information is structured, while the notes are freeform, making Zotero an excellent blend of the two styles of information gathering. To be useful, of course, you must be able to find the records again. We will begin with the filing system that mimics but dramatically improves upon your old-fashioned filing cabinets.

ORGANIZING RESEARCH COLLECTIONS

4

Zotero's collection structure in the left-most pane of your desktop workspace becomes your filing system—your organizational structure. It allows you to group materials in the way that best serves your research needs. It gives you everything your file cabinets did and then so many things you regretted they could not do.

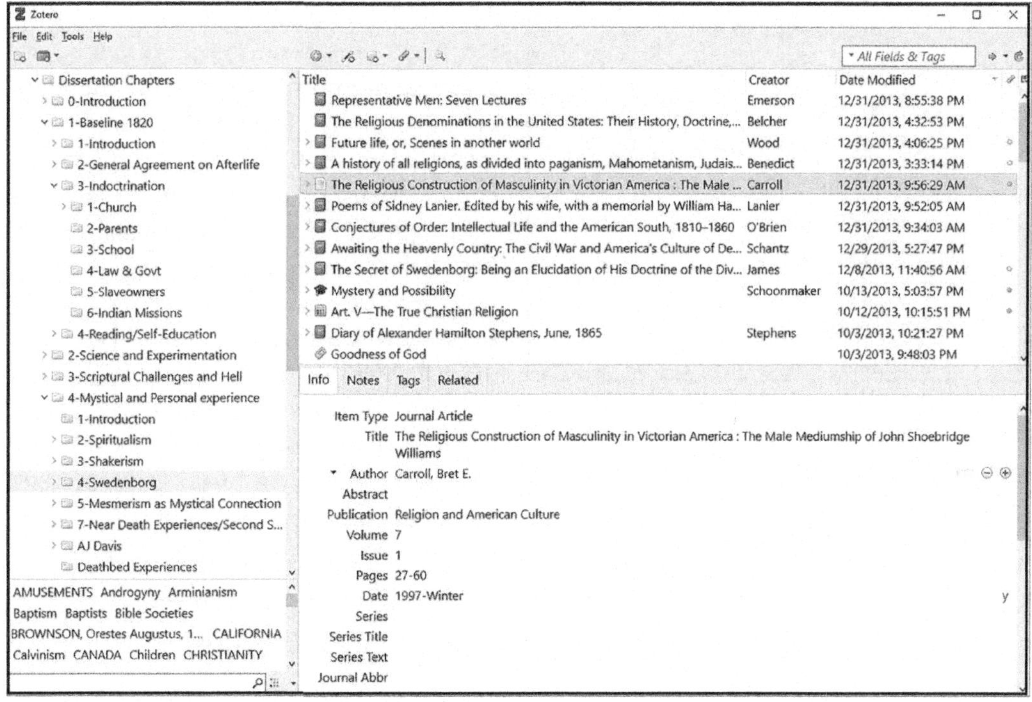

The Collection structure becomes your filing cabinet, binder, writing outline, or all of these at the same time.

USING ZOTERO COLLECTIONS

A collection is a container for research items that need to be stored together. It can serve the purpose of a manila folder. Or a binder. Or a file box. Or a file drawer. It can organize the chapter or the lecture you are writing, replacing the old-fashioned index cards you used to keep. You can make it as small or as large as you need it to be—as simple or as complex.

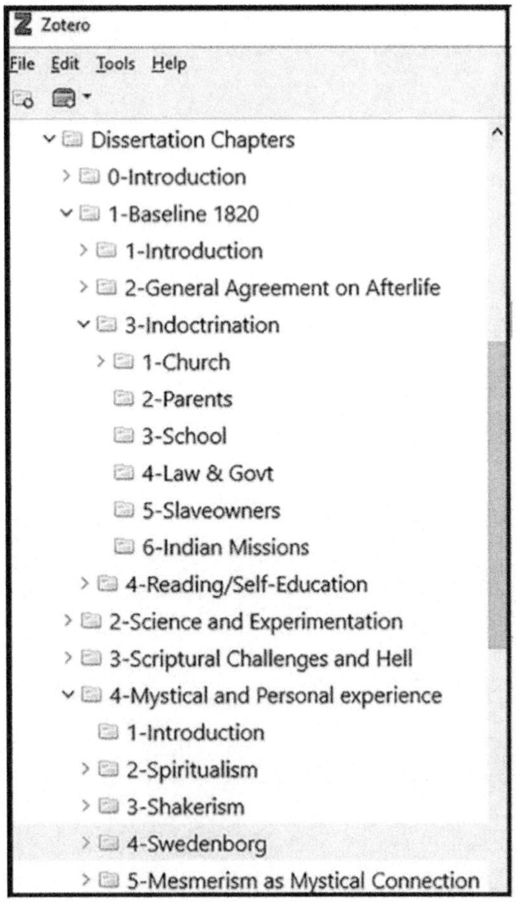

Zotero sorts its collections in alphabetical order. It handles your files in much the same way we all commonly do in a file cabinet and the way our computer file management systems usually sort files. If you have a set of folders you want to sort in a way other than alphabetically, use a numeral at the start of the collection name.

As you see in the image, I sorted my dissertation research in order by the chapters and sections I intended to cover, using numbers to make them fall in the desired order. If I changed my mind about the order, I changed the numbers. To change the name of a collection, you right-click or double-click on the collection name and type the new text.

If you want to force a collection to the top, begin the name with a symbol (my preference is an underscore). If you want to force one to the absolute end, no matter how many folders you create in between, start the collection name with "zzz" or something similar.

Collections automatically sort in alphanumeric order. If the order needs to fall in something other than alphabetical order, use numerals to force the order you desire.

Exercise 3: Create a collection

You have already created your first collection when you copied your sample data to *My Library* in Chapter 2. Rarely, though, will you create your collections by that method. Here is the normal method:

Step 1 Go to *My Library* (top-most item in your Collections pane), right-click, and select **New Collection**. Or, you can click on it and use the New Collection button on the toolbar.

Step 2 In the popup window, type "FAMILY HISTORY," and click **OK**.

Zotero will add the collection above your sample data folder. You can then begin to populate your *FAMILY HISTORY* folder with subfolders Zotero calls "subcollections."

Exercise 4: Create a subcollection

Subcollections are any folders nested inside of the folders (collections) you have created under *My Library*.

Step 1 Go to your new *FAMILY HISTORY* collection, right-click, and select **New Subcollection**. Or, you can click on it and use the New Collection button on the toolbar.

Step 2 In the popup window, type "PEOPLE," and click **OK**.

You can repeat this procedure to create more subcollections under *FAMILY HISTORY* or to nest deeper layers of folders under PEOPLE. Your subfolders may be family surnames, in which you might have individual names. You will be able to nest deeper and deeper layers of folders if it is helpful to your research organization. (We will talk more about genealogical organization in Chapter 10.)

For help in moving around in your growing collection and its subsets, you can collapse subcollections from view. To the left of each folder, you will see an arrow, turned either right (>), indicating that there is a set of folders hidden beneath the one displayed, or downward (V), which displays the subfolders. Click on the arrow to open and close the containing folder.

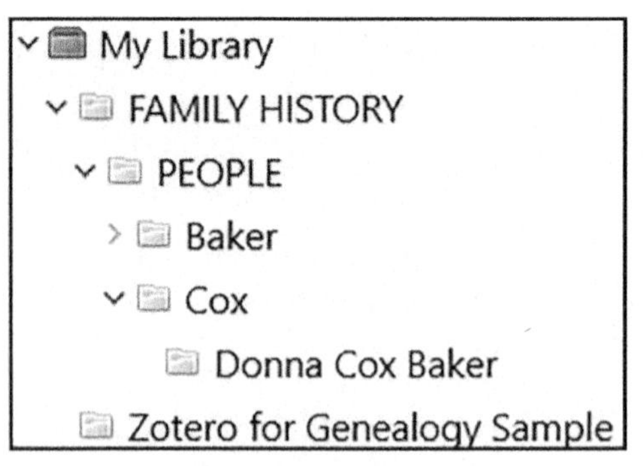

Arrows to the left of subcollection titles can collapse and expand the available contents

Research records inside collection folders

In reality, every research record you add to Zotero exists in only one place: *My Library*. As you add the items to the various collections, the research records look and behave as though they reside inside the collection. But the records you see inside a collection are in actuality virtual links to the main record in *My Library*. Any changes you appear to make to the item in the collection folder, you are making to the main record.

Exercise 5: Testing the virtual links to *My Library*

Let's test out this idea of the "virtual link" that allows a research record to appear to be in multiple folders or collections when it really only exists once.

Step 1 Click on *My Library* in your Collections pane. All of your current research records will be displayed in the Research List. Click on the item labeled "The Beyond Kin Project." Notice that the Abstract field is empty.

Step 2 In your Collections pane, click on *Zotero for Genealogy Sample Data*. Now click the same entry, "The Beyond Kin Project," in that list. It appears to be a duplicate of the one you saw in *My Library*.

Step 3 In the Abstract field, type your own name.

Step 4 Click on *My Library* again, and then click on "The Beyond Kin Project." The Abstract field should now have your name in it.

As you can see, the collections appear to have duplicate records. However, only one actually exists—the one in *My Library*. The seeming duplicate in *Zotero for Genealogy Sample Data* is a virtual link to the original record. If you change it here, you are changing the main record.

This is a great benefit over the traditional filing in paper systems and even in most other notetaking software. This allows you to find a desired research record in multiple folders, though it exists only once. As you add notes, correct errors, or otherwise improve the record, your changes will appear wherever the record is used.

Exercise 6: Add the record to another folder

Let's say you also want the record discussed above to show up in the new folder you created—your *FAMILY HISTORY* folder.

Step 1 In the Research List of *My Library*, click and drag "The Beyond Kin Project" over to the *FAMILY HISTORY* folder. When the folder is highlighted, drop the file there. Notice that "The Beyond Kin Project" record is still sitting in *My Library*.

Step 2 Click on *FAMILY HISTORY*. The collection now has a single record, also "The Beyond Kin Project." It is a virtual link to the main record, not a separate copy. You can add a virtual link to this record in as many collections or folders as you like.

If you want to remove it from one collection, right-click it there, and choose to **Remove Item from Collection.** If instead, you choose to **Remove Item to Trash**, you will be removing the research record from all locations, including *My Library*. (It will remain in Zotero's trash bin until you manually choose to empty the trash.)

Moving Subcollections

The subcollections within a particular collection folder will organize themselves in alphabetical order, as discussed. But you can move the folder into or out of another folder easily.

Drag the folder you want to move until it is on top of and highlighting the folder where you want it to be. Drop it there, and it will be copied, along with all its contents, and placed in the proper place in the new folder based on its name in alphabetical order. Remove it from the original folder by right-clicking and choosing **Remove item from collection**.

Deleting Collections and Subcollections

If you want to remove a collection folder from Zotero, you may do it one of two ways. Right-click the folder and choose one of the following options:

Delete Collection
If you choose this option, Zotero will delete the collection folder and any subcollection folders within it. But the research records you had in the collection folders will continue to exist in *My Library* and in any collections with virtual links to the item. The folders will not be available from Zotero's trash bin.

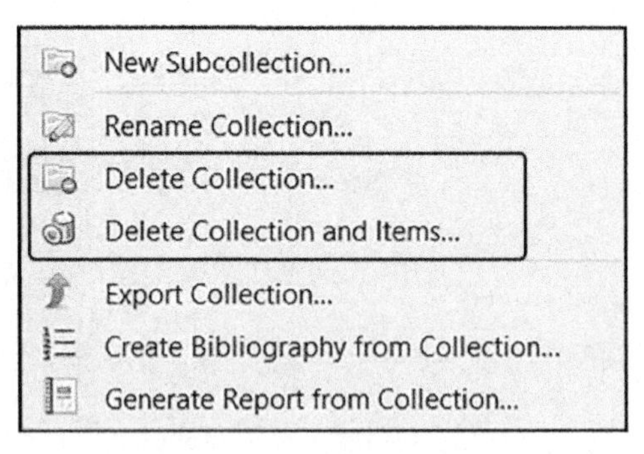

You can choose to delete a collection with or without its contents.

Delete Collection and Items
This option will delete the selected collection folder, all subcollection folders, and all research records they contained. The folders may not be recovered from the trash, but the research records can be recovered until you empty the trash bin.

Summary

Zotero's collection structure allows you to organize data in the way that works best for you. Even better, it allows you to file something multiple different ways without duplicating the information in reality. Next, we will look at another feature that mimics old filing systems without the pitfalls. Attachments allow you to store all sorts of documents and files along with the citation records and notes you will take.

MANAGING YOUR ATTACHMENTS

5

Zotero's handling of attachments extends its power and value to you in many ways. You can store PDFs, text and document files, spreadsheets, photographs, music, audio, and other types of files. This allows Zotero to replace your file cabinet for all but the collectible photographs, valuable original documents, and certified copies you *want* to keep in an original form.

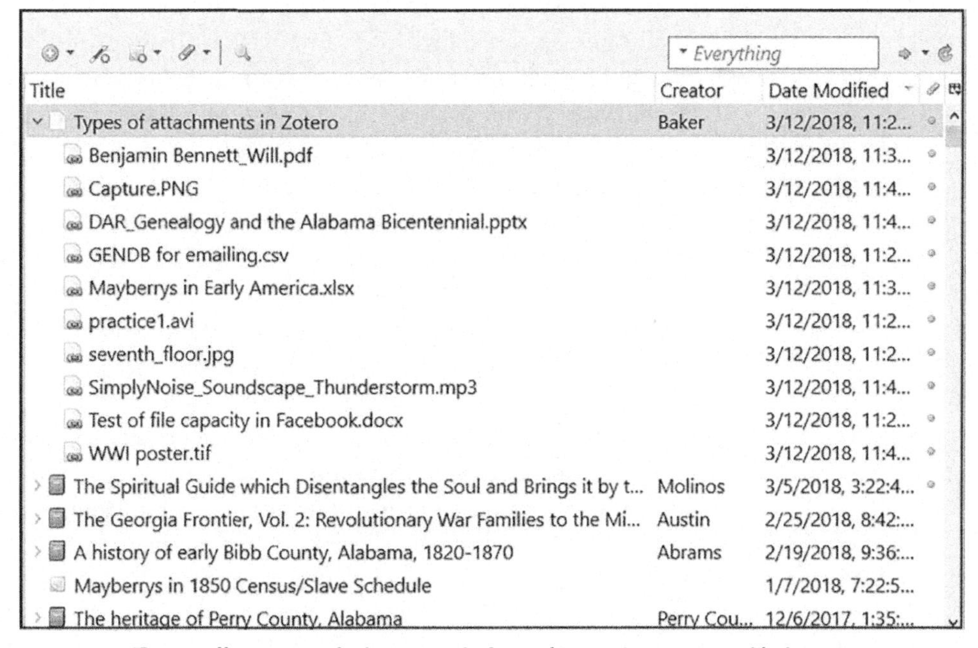

Zotero allows you to link to or embed attachments in numerous file formats, attaching multiple files to a single research record, if desired, as shown above.

How you set up and manage your attachments can determine the amount of space needed to sync to the Zotero cloud. It will determine whether you will use Zotero to back up all of your data or blend Zotero with another storage option. Choices about attachments will also determine the degree to which you can search within your attachments (another remarkable asset of Zotero).

You can attach files to any research record. You can attach as many files as you need to a single research record. The attachments can reside inside Zotero or you can link to them externally on your own hard drive, external drive, or other storage option.

Before You Start Attaching

There are a few important things to know about attachments before you start to use them. You will want to make your choices about attachments with long-term storage in mind—and the many variables that long-term *anything* brings to our decisions.

Embedded versus linked attachments

Zotero allows you to embed a copy of your attachments into its database or to create links to them in external locations. While the two options will operate very much the same in your daily use of your research, this choice will affect the size of your Zotero database.

If you choose to link to attachments in external locations, the 300 MB of free cloud space Zotero offers can last a very long time—assuming you are not pasting images into your notes. I have used Zotero for years, accumulating 5,300 research records as of now, with only 56% of my free Zotero storage used.

I protect my external attachments using cloud storage options I already have in place for other purposes. This ensures that my attachments are being backed up to a location outside my home—something we should all do with our genealogical digital resources. This also allows me to access my attachments remotely, even when I am using someone else's computer without Zotero installed.

If you choose instead to store full copies of your attachments in Zotero, syncing everything to the Zotero cloud, be aware that your 300 MB of free storage will run out quickly. A high-resolution image of a single map can be larger than that. You will want to choose Zotero's option for unlimited storage, which currently costs $10 per month. With this option, your research records and attachments will be perpetually backed up and accessible remotely.

Zotero Storage

Account · Profile · C.V. · Privacy · Email · Feeds/API · Storage

Frequently Asked Questions

Current Plan	
Quota	300 MB
Expiration	Never
Current Usage	My Library - 169.1 MB
	Total - 169.1 MB
	56.4%

Change Plan		
Storage Amount	Annual Price (USD)	
300 MB	Free	
2 GB	$20	Select Plan
6 GB	$60	Select Plan
Unlimited	$120	Select Plan

Zotero offers 300 MB of free storage space to sync and access your data remotely.

Searching the contents of attachments

One feature that makes Zotero an exceptional resource is its ability to search the contents of many attachments—even when you have chosen to link to them externally. Even better, it indexes the contents, making the searches remarkably quick. It can search plain text files and searchable PDFs.

Plain text files are a type of document containing only simple text, with no formatting. You may save them as the "Plain Text" type of document in your word processing software. Or you might create them in a plain text editor like Microsoft Notepad. They typically have a .txt extension, if your computer displays extensions.

More useful for most of us, Zotero can search for a particular string of text in attached PDF files that have a searchable text layer. It is important to distinguish a searchable PDF from one that merely looks like it should be. Some PDFs are actually just a snapshot of text. Your eyes can process the letters as words, but a computer simply sees ink unless an invisible text layer hides behind the image of the page. There is a quick way to tell if your document is readable as text. Click on a word on the PDF page. If the PDF puts a cursor into the word or selects the word, your PDF should be searchable. If instead, the entire page is highlighted, the page is not searchable.

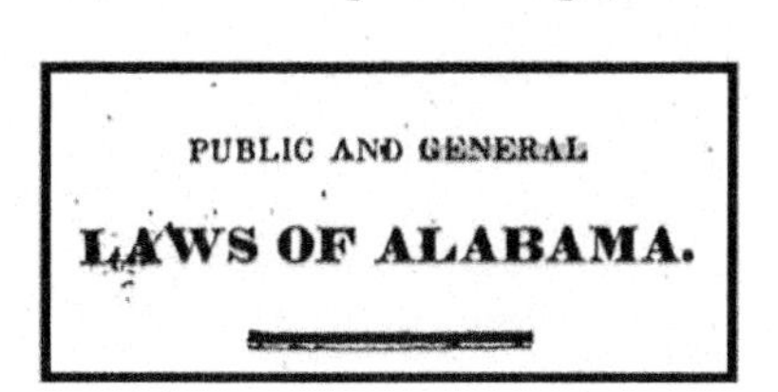
PUBLIC AND GENERAL

LAWS OF ALABAMA.

The word "General" has been highlighted when double-clicked, indicating this is a searchable PDF.

Some PDF software can convert the images of words into real text by a process called Optical Character Recognition, or OCR. OCR is not always perfect in its translation, but even a bad OCR scan can sometimes be helpful in making your document findable.

Many other document types—including rich-text documents (like your standard Microsoft Word document) and spreadsheets—can be saved as searchable PDFs. This will allow you to make most attachments searchable, if desired. If you also want to have access to the document in its native form, you can create a link to the PDF and then also create a link to the original file.

Setting a base directory and relative path for linked attachments

If you choose to link to your attachments externally, rather than storing them in Zotero, think carefully about where you store them and how you name them on your hard drive or external drive. As you browse and link to the attachments, you are essentially giving Zotero an address where it can find them—a path. If you later delete, rename, or move the attachment on your drive, Zotero's link will be broken.

You cannot guarantee, even if you are very careful, that you will always be able to keep your attachment files in exactly the same place. Computers become obsolete or damaged. Operating systems are upgraded, forcing unexpected changes. We die and leave our research to descendants. Things change. You want to be able to easily move your attachment files from one place to another without breaking the links you have created to the original address.

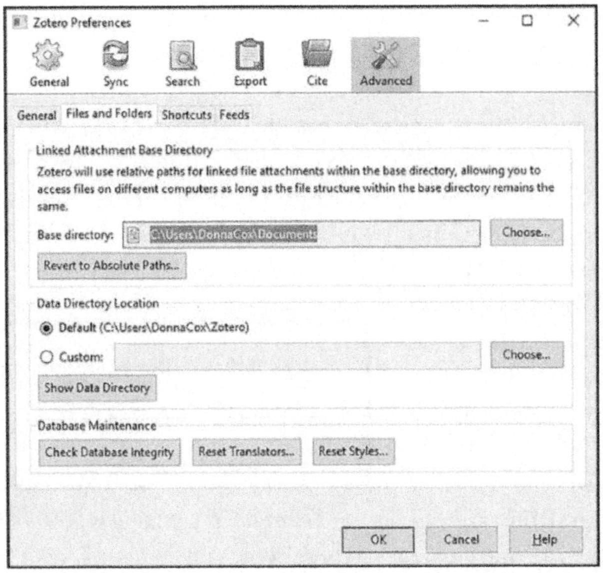

Organize linked attachments in whatever way you wish—so long as they remain in the same path relative to your Base directory.

Zotero offers a way to handle major file movements by allowing you to designate a "base directory," with all of your files organized relative to it. You tell Zotero what your base directory is in Preferences—Advanced—Files and Folders. If for any reason you want to move all of your files to a new location—a new computer, an external hard drive, a cloud location—you can move them all intact to a new base directory and tell Zotero what the new location is.

As you see in the image above, my base directory is

C:\Users\DonnaCox\Documents

Within this base directory, I have created a file to hold all my genealogy-related files, including the attachments to which Zotero is linked. I call the file "Genealogy," which has the path "C:\Users\DonnaCox\Documents\Genealogy" on my computer.

Inside the Genealogy folder, I organize everything as I want it. I use subfolders called "PEOPLE"," "PLACES," "TOOLS," and "TOPICS" to store attachments. Underneath "PEOPLE," I have a folder for every family surname, and under that a folder for every person, and so on. (I will talk more about this system in Chapter 10.)

The important thing is to have a system and stick to it. Your base directory can change, but everything stored beneath it must keep its same order and filenames to preserve the links. This creates a "relative path" for Zotero. Your attachment is always in the same place, *relative* to the base directory.

Let's say I have decided to move all my attachments to an external hard drive that is assigned the drive letter D by my computer. Zotero is still looking for all of the attachments at the old location, and I could break hundreds or thousands of links by moving the files, without designating a base directory. Let's say I assign a new base directory of:

D:\Zotero\Attachments

I then get the Genealogy folder from the old location and copy or move it to *D:\Zotero\Attachments*. My attachments are now all in subfolders of "D:\Zotero\Attachments\Genealogy\". When I click on an attachment link in Zotero, it knows to look in "D:\Zotero\Attachments\" rather than "C:\Users\DonnaCox-\Documents\". So long as everything within the Genealogy folder remains in exactly the same structure it already had, Zotero will find it.

CREATING FILE ATTACHMENTS

In Zotero, all attachments can stand alone or be linked to a research citation record, not to a note or another attachment. In your Research List pane, you will right-click on the citation record, and choose **Add attachment**. You will then choose one of the following three options:

- Attach link to URI
- Attach stored copy of file
- Attach link to file

Attach link to URI

You might have a reason to link your research record to other dynamic resources—online and otherwise. The Uniform Resource Indicator (URI) link can be a resource name recognizable to certain protocols or it can be the online location of the resource.

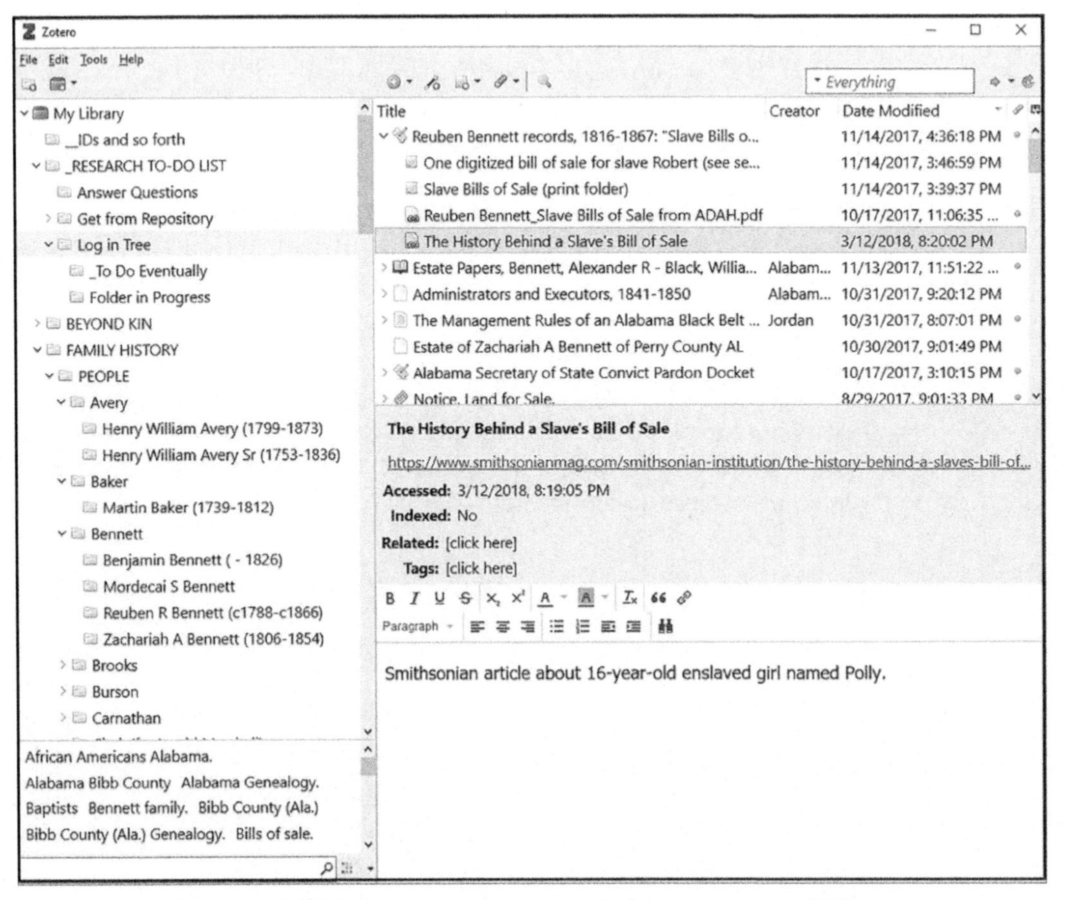

Using the URI link, you can create a meaningful connection to a URL or other resources, using a descriptive title and notes.

For our purposes, most use of this attachment link will be in the form of the Uniform Resource Locator (URL), which is a type of URI that creates a path to the desired resource. In creating a URL, add the link and a meaningful title, which will become the label that Zotero displays in the attachment list for your record.

You already have a URL field in your research citation, which will serve you perfectly well in most cases. But this link allows you to identify multiple resources online that support your research. You can also create a note attached to the URL link, expanding its meaningfulness to you.

In the case of URI links, Zotero will only search what you have typed into the title or the notes. It will not search the contents of the resource to which you are linking. Therefore, you might want to add a few defining terms in the title that will help you to find your way back to this resource.

Exercise 7: Create a URL attachment

Let's say you want to create a link to Elizabeth Shown Mills's website, supporting *Evidence Explained*. You want to attach the link to the citation you have created for the book. Follow these steps:

Step 1 Click on the *Zotero for Genealogy Sample Data* collection in your Collections pane.

Step 2 In your Research List, find the second copy of the *Evidence Explained* research record you created, and right-click on it.

Step 3 In the displayed menu, move your cursor to **Add attachments**, which will display a submenu. In the submenu, select **Attach link to URI**.

Step 4 Enter https://www.evidenceexplained.com in the Link field.

Step 5 In the Title field, type "Evidence Explained website with Sample QuickCheck Models" and click **OK**.

Step 6 Double-click on the new link under your *Evidence Explained* record, and you should see the website open for you.

You have created a very convenient way to access the website, but you have also added an element that was missing. By using the words "QuickCheck Model" in the title, you have made this record findable if you search on "QuickCheck," even if you have forgotten the name of the book or author.

Attach stored copy of file

You may attach a copy of a file to your research record so that it becomes a part of Zotero's data. If you are syncing your files to Zotero's online cloud storage, your attachments will be synced, along with your research citation records. See "Copied versus linked attachments" above, for a cautionary discussion of the cloud space needed.

Attach link to file

This option (my personal favorite) allows you to simply point Zotero to an attachment stored on your computer or another external location. It makes the file quickly accessible from Zotero but keeps it separate from Zotero's main data storage. It will not be synced to Zotero's cloud with the citation records. If you are already syncing your genealogy to cloud storage other than Zotero, you will likely find this the desirable option. See "Copied versus linked attachments," above, for more information. If you link to a searchable PDF or text file, Zotero will include the text of your attachment in its searches.

The last two attachment options are created in virtually the same way, browsing to find the desired attachment on your hard drive or other device. And from your perspective, they will look and operate almost identically in Zotero. You can only tell them apart by the icon Zotero uses. If you chose **Attach link to file**, there will be an icon of a document with chain links on top of it. If you chose **Attach stored copy of file**, you will see an icon of a plain document.

The most significant difference between the two will be happening behind the scenes. If you chose **Attach stored copy of file**, your Zotero file increased in size by the disk space that the file takes up. And if you are syncing your data to Zotero's cloud, the new file will be taking up some of your space allocation there. If you chose **Attach link to file**, Zotero has only added to its girth a short string of text pointing to a file that already sits on your own device. And when you sync, that small text string, not an entire document, will move to Zotero's cloud.

Exercise 8: Attach a PDF

To test Zotero's ability to attach documents and to prepare for later exercises, let's pull a PDF from the web to attach to an item in your *Zotero for Genealogy Sample Data* folder.

Step 1 In your web browser, go the following URL: https://gegbound.com/PDFsample.pdf. (This is case-sensitive.)

Step 2 Download the PDF to your computer, either by right-clicking in the screen and selecting **Save As** or by using the Download button on your screen (which probably looks like a down arrow pointing to an underscore). Store it in a place you can remember.

Step 3 In Zotero, select *Zotero for Genealogy Sample Data* folder in the upper Collections pane. Then click on an existing research item labeled **Descriptive Pamphlet of Hillsborough, Florida . . . .**

Step 4 Right-click on the pamphlet item and click **Add Attachment—Attach Link to File**. Find the PDF you just saved to your computer and select it. It will now appear beneath the pamphlet item in your Research List.

RESTORING BROKEN ATTACHMENT LINKS

Inevitably, you will occasionally find—or even consciously cause—a broken link to an attachment. While the relative path described above in the section titled "Setting a relative path for linked attachments," will eliminate major breakage, you will occasionally move or rename a file, accidentally or on purpose.

If a link has been broken, you will know it when you attempt to open the attachment and see this message:

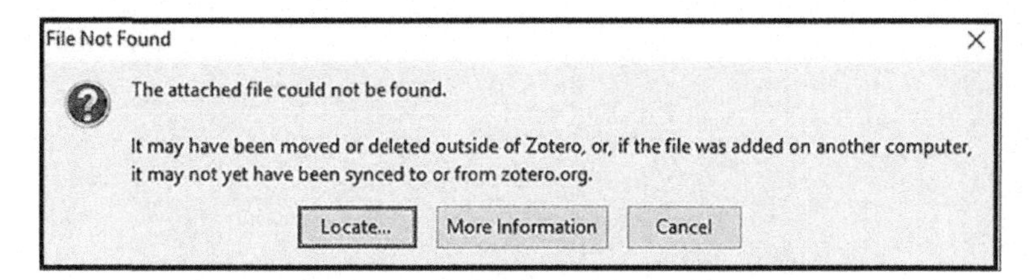

A file that has been renamed or moved will generate this error. Click ***Locate*** *to find and reconnect the file.*

Click **Locate** to search for the missing attachment. Zotero will restore the link when you have located the file.

SUMMARY

Attachments are the bulk of what once filled our file cabinets. The simple act of shifting the old paper burden to a digital form on your hard drive offers a great improvement. But by attaching them to Zotero's research records, they become so much more usable than our paper files ever were. Zotero makes them eminently more usable, in no small part because it makes them so much more *findable*. In the next chapter, we will talk about the many ways Zotero helps us find the proverbial "needle in a haystack."

SEARCHING, SORTING AND FINDING YOUR RESEARCH

6

As our research records grow from hundreds to thousands to potentially tens of thousands, *finding* them again is the key to successful research and analysis. Zotero creates multiple layers of findability, ensuring the best possible success in making your research count.

BASIC SORTING

Zotero allows you to sort a selected collection on any of the displayed fields in your research list. If you have selected *My Library* in your collections list, you are sorting your entire collection. Sort the records by clicking on the heading of the column that holds the values you want to sort.

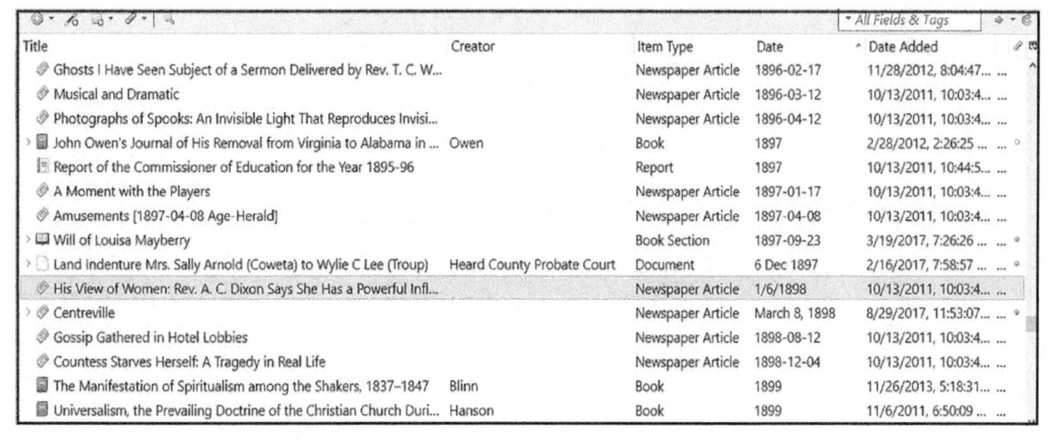

Title	Creator	Item Type	Date	Date Added
Ghosts I Have Seen Subject of a Sermon Delivered by Rev. T. C. W...		Newspaper Article	1896-02-17	11/28/2012, 8:04:47...
Musical and Dramatic		Newspaper Article	1896-03-12	10/13/2011, 10:03:4...
Photographs of Spooks: An Invisible Light That Reproduces Invisi...		Newspaper Article	1896-04-12	10/13/2011, 10:03:4...
John Owen's Journal of His Removal from Virginia to Alabama in ...	Owen	Book	1897	2/28/2012, 2:26:25 ...
Report of the Commissioner of Education for the Year 1895-96		Report	1897	10/13/2011, 10:44:5...
A Moment with the Players		Newspaper Article	1897-01-17	10/13/2011, 10:03:4...
Amusements [1897-04-08 Age-Herald]		Newspaper Article	1897-04-08	10/13/2011, 10:03:4...
Will of Louisa Mayberry		Book Section	1897-09-23	3/19/2017, 7:26:26 ...
Land Indenture Mrs. Sally Arnold (Coweta) to Wylie C Lee (Troup)	Heard County Probate Court	Document	6 Dec 1897	2/16/2017, 7:58:57 ...
His View of Women: Rev. A. C. Dixon Says She Has a Powerful Infl...		Newspaper Article	1/6/1898	10/13/2011, 10:03:4...
Centreville		Newspaper Article	March 8, 1898	8/29/2017, 11:53:07...
Gossip Gathered in Hotel Lobbies		Newspaper Article	1898-08-12	10/13/2011, 10:03:4...
Countess Starves Herself: A Tragedy in Real Life		Newspaper Article	1898-12-04	10/13/2011, 10:03:4...
The Manifestation of Spiritualism among the Shakers, 1837–1847	Blinn	Book	1899	11/26/2013, 5:18:31...
Universalism, the Prevailing Doctrine of the Christian Church Duri...	Hanson	Book	1899	11/6/2011, 6:50:09 ...

The data has been sorted in order by the Date value.

Clicking a column heading a second time will reverse the sort order. Fields with no values will be sorted to the low end of the sorted range.

When sorting the Date field, Zotero will not sort the records in numerical or alphabetical order. It will arrange the material in proper date order, based on its understanding of your date format. Therefore, though your database might include a mixture of date formats—1/5/1854, 5 January 1854, Jan 5, 1854, and 1854-01-05 all being the same date—Zotero knows where they belong in the larger sorted collection.

CHOOSING AND CONTROLLING COLUMNS

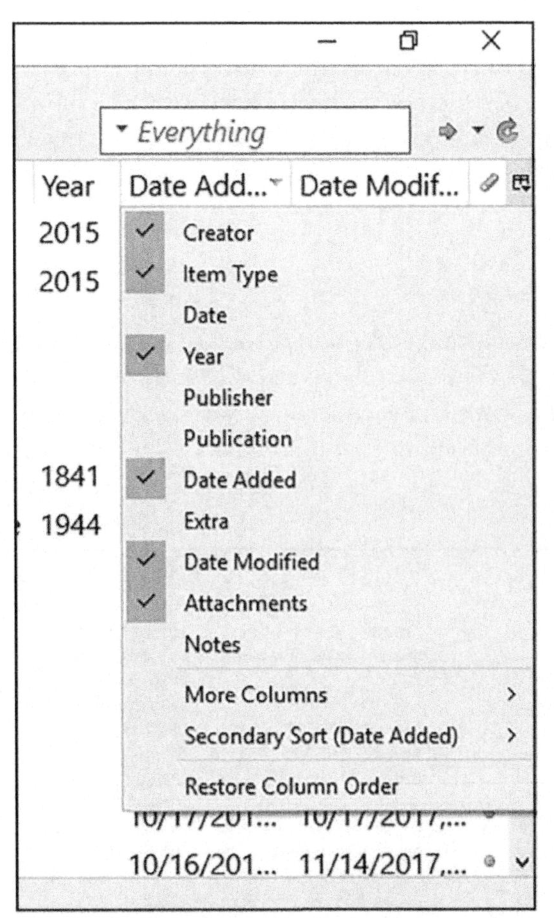

You may add, resize, and rearrange columns in the Zotero research list.

You can choose the available columns to display in your research list, which

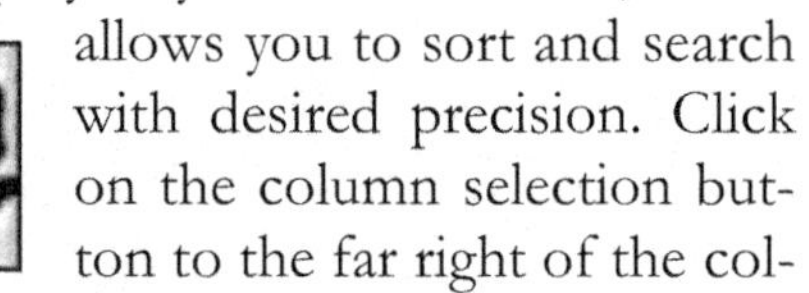

allows you to sort and search with desired precision. Click on the column selection button to the far right of the column headings to choose the fields you want to display.

The most commonly used fields display at the top of the selection list, but many others are available in the **More Columns** option. You are also able to choose a **Secondary Sort** field.

You may resize the columns by dragging the thin gray line between the column headings to the right or left. You can rearrange the columns by clicking and dragging the heading label, dropping it where you want the column to be.

Exercise 9: Add, arrange, and remove column in research list

To practice these skills, let's sort your research records by their item type. You will make it your first column, sort by it, and then remove it. Click on your *Zotero for Genealogy Sample Data* collection and follow these steps:

Step 1 You need to put the Item Type column into your display. In the top-right corner of your Research List pane, click on the column selection button.

Step 2 Choose **Item Type** from the displayed list.

Step 3 The item type now shows in your list, probably not in the first position. Click and hold the **Item Type** label above the new column and drag it to the left until you drop it on top of the first field—probably your Title. The Item Type should now be your first column.

Step 4 Click on the **Item Type** label to sort your records by Item Type order.

Step 5 To remove the Item Type column, now that you're done with the exercise, click again on your column selection button and choose **Item Type**, this time deselecting it. Or, if you prefer, from the same list, choose **Restore Column Order** to take your entire list back to its original form.

BASIC SEARCHING

Zotero offers a search box above the Research List pane, which gives several options for filtering the search. You do not have to recall exact phrases. Zotero will find any record that contains the terms you enter in the field, regardless of the order of the search terms or the fields in which those terms exist. You have three research options:

Title, Creator, Year
Zotero will search only the three most commonly populated fields in your citation records: the title, the author or creator, and the publication or creation year.

All Fields & Tags
Zotero will seek your search terms in any citation field or in the tags you have assigned.

Everything
Zotero will search all citation fields, tags, notes, PDFs and text files for your search terms.

Zotero's basic search function can look for any of your search terms, filtering the search in basic ways.

ADVANCED SEARCHING

You can search with greater precision by using Zotero's Advanced Search feature. You access it by clicking on the icon of a magnifying glass on the toolbar.

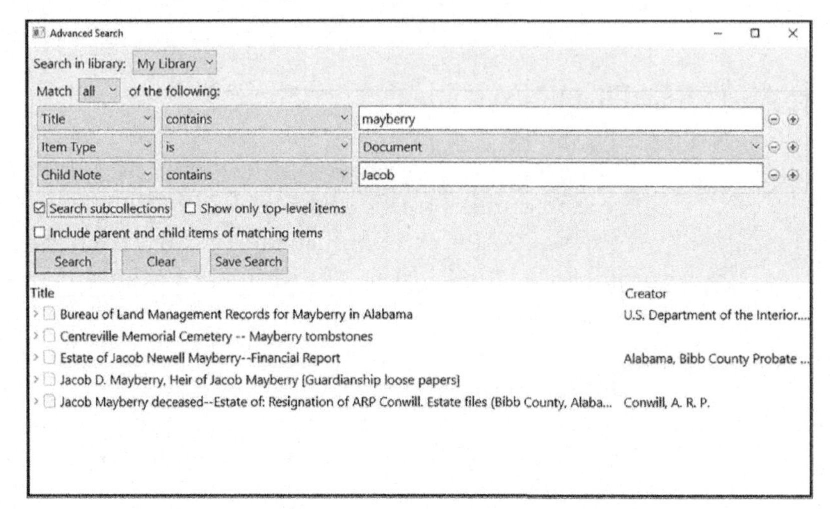

Zotero's Advanced Search feature allows you to get very specific in searching for an elusive record.

You can create multiple criteria, choosing to retrieve records that match any or all of your specified criteria. You may seek a specific word or phrase within a specific field. You can have Zotero choose records that do *not* have a specific word or phrase in a specific field. And you can save a search to use again, if helpful.

The search criteria can contain from one to many elements—each further expanding or refining the set of records Zotero will retrieve. You add or remove criteria lines using the minus and plus icons at the end of a displayed line.

With each line, you will choose the field to search, the evaluation option, and the content you are evaluating in your search.

Field

The field element is chosen from a drop-down list of all available fields in your research records, including collections, tags, and notes.

Evaluation Option

The evaluation option is chosen from a drop-down list that changes, depending on the field you chose in the first element. If you are evaluating the Notes field, for example, your options will be "contains" and "does not contain." The Creator field includes both of those, but adds "is" and "is not," so you can evaluate the entire contents of the field. Date fields will allow you to evaluate before and after criteria, including whether the record contains a date within a certain number of days, months, or years before the current date.

Content

In the content element, you might be presented with a drop-down list or a text box, depending upon the type of field you are searching. Here, you tell Zotero what information you want it to retrieve (or avoid) in the selected field, as it chooses the records to retrieve for your review.

You may further refine what Zotero finds and how it displays what it finds by clicking on any of these options:

☑ Search subcollections ☐ Show only top-level items
☐ Include parent and child items of matching items

Search subcollections
In most cases, you will be searching your entire data set, the *My Library* collection, for which this option has no use. But if you choose a specific collection to search (by selecting "Collection" as your field element on one of your criteria lines), this option will allow you to specify whether the subcollections within that collection will be included.

Show only top-level items
This option controls how the retrieved records will display. If this field is selected, Zotero will show only the research records in which the primary record contains the specified content. It will not pull child records attached to the primary record. If it is not selected, Zotero will display the entire set of research items associated with the matching record—its parent or child records, if available, and any other records attached to its parent. Zotero will display the item that contains the matching record in full resolution. The other items will be faded, but visible.

Include parent and child items of matching items
If this is selected, Zotero treats the parent of a matching child record the same way it treats the child. Both will be displayed in full resolution. If you have selected this and selected the Show only top-level items option, only the parent records will be displayed.

Saved searches

If you click the **Save Search** button, Zotero will create an item in your Collections pane, and allow you to give it a name. This allows you to repeat a search easily, showing the retrieved records within in the main desktop view, rather than in the Advanced Search popup window. Your saved searches will appear as a folder icon with a magnifying glass in the Collections pane.

Land in Notes Search
Tablet Files

Exercise 10: Do an advanced search

Admittedly, we have so little data in Zotero at present that a complex search might seem a waste of time. But let's do it anyway, in preparation for the day that you, like me, have 5,000 items in your database—many entered years ago and no longer remembered well, if at all. Let's say you have collected hundreds of maps and hundreds of books and articles about maps. You want to pinpoint actual maps you have of Louisiana in the early nineteenth century. Do the following:

Step 1 Click *My Library* in the Collections pane, which will open this search to everything in your Zotero database.

Step 2 Click on the Advanced Search icon on the toolbar, which will bring up the search criteria window.

Step 3 Fill out your Advanced Search window as you see below—using the plus-sign button to the right of the first criteria line to add more lines—and click **Search**. Zotero will display the one map you have in your sample data. You can go to that record by double-clicking, but let's say you are going to be collecting a number of these maps and want to be able to repeat the search….

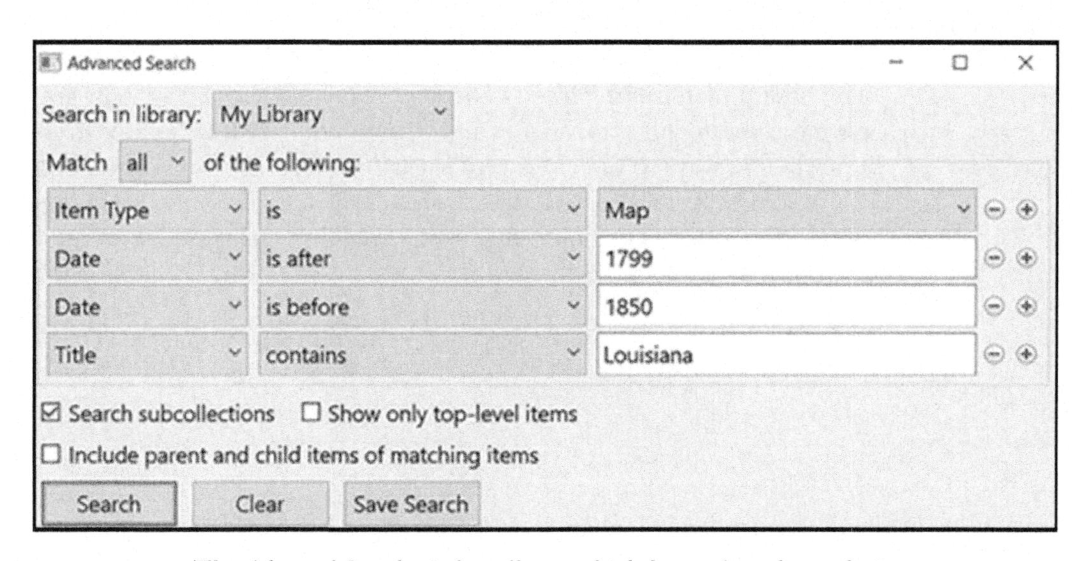

The Advanced Search window allows multiple layers of search complexity.

Step 4 To make this search available again later, click the **Save Search** button. Enter a meaningful label like "Early 19th-century LA maps," and click **OK**. You will now have an item toward the bottom of the *My Library* portion of your Collections pane. Click on it at any time to bring your search up in your Research List.

TAGS

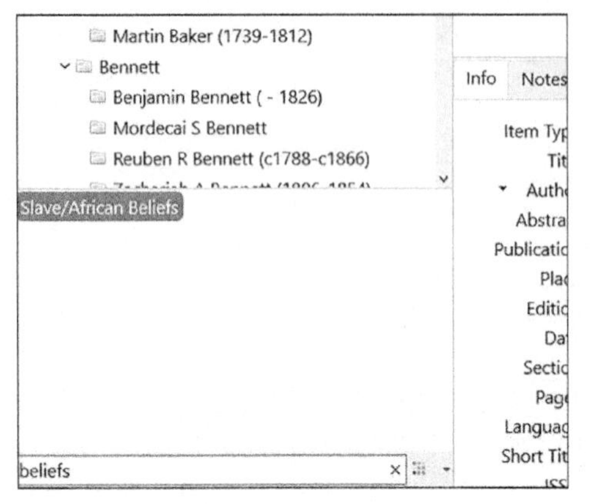

You can filter available tags by entering keywords in the search box.

You can bring up all of the research items with a particular tag by using the Tag pane in the bottom left corner of your desktop workspace. By default, Zotero displays all available tags. To reduce the options to a particular subset of tags, type a term in the search box at the bottom of the window.

The dotted icon to the right of the search box allows you to restore the full set of tags if you have isolated to a specific selection. It also allows you to hide "automatic tags," those created when bibliographic research items are imported from your web browser. You may also delete these automatic tags.

SUMMARY

The ability to retrieve records you have entered becomes vitally important as your collection grows and your memory fades. Zotero offers a number of ways to find your way back to exactly the source you need.

You now have reviewed all of Zotero's most commonly used functions. We move next to several add-on programs that magnify its value to your research.

PART II:
ZOTERO ADD-ONS

Zotero is "open source" software, allowing its own personnel or other organizations or individuals to build extra features onto the application. There are many such "add-ons," but I will describe the three I have used for years with great success.

The first two, "Zotero Connector" and "Zotero Word Processor Plug-in," are supported by Zotero. The other one, "ZotFile," programmed by Joscha Legewie, offers excellent tools for enhancing the use of PDFs.

You can find many other tools available on Zotero's website, though they are not created or supported by Zotero. You need to be aware that you use them at your own risk, and many may be well worth the risk. Some require programming knowledge to implement. You can examine the list at

https://www.zotero.org/support/plugins

Zotero Connectors & Instant Data Entry 7

The Zotero Connector first hooked me on the Zotero product, making it unbeatable in my opinion. It is a plug-in for use in your Internet browser, to capture bibliographic data from a web page, entering it into Zotero with the push of a button. With thousands of bibliographic citations to enter while working on my dissertation, this saved me hundreds of hours and much aggravation.

Installing Zotero Connector

Zotero offers connectors to Chrome, Firefox, and Safari web browsers, specifically, and also has a "bookmarklet" for any other browser, smartphone, or tablet.* The Zotero Connectors can all be downloaded from the Zotero website by choosing **Install Browser Connector** from your Tools menu.

I use the Chrome browser, so the instructions here will be for Chrome. If you prefer another browser, look for a link on the screen saying, **Show all connectors**.

For Chrome, select **Install Chrome Connector**. For all other browsers, select **Zotero Connectors for other browsers** and follow Zotero's instructions for your particular browser. Assuming you are operating from within Chrome as you do this, you will see a notification about adding the extension to the browser environment. Choose **Add extension**.

* The operation of bookmarklets will vary, depending upon the environment. Search Zotero's online forums for details about your own device and software.

Your Chrome browser will give you a second notice that the extension has been added, and a tiny icon will now appear at the top line of your browser window, just to the right of your URL field. The icon will change shapes, depending upon what type of information Zotero perceives to be displayed on the screen. If you are on an informational website it will look like a computer screen. If you are looking at a book advertisement on Amazon, it will look like a book. Let your cursor rest on top of it, and if you see the words "Save to Zotero," you have located the proper icon.

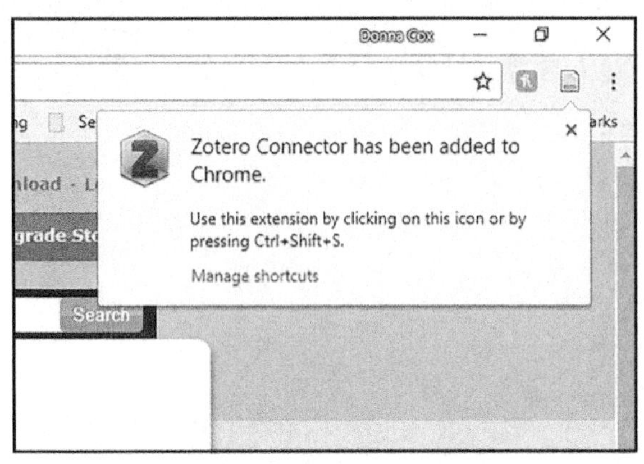

The Zotero Connector adds a new icon to your browser window for capturing citations to Zotero.

This icon will become your method to populate your Zotero research records with citation information someone *else* had to type. You will love the work it saves.

Using the Zotero Connector

Your Zotero software must be open in the background for Zotero Connector to operate properly. You can use Zotero Connector on any page displayed in the browser you chose to enable with the plug-in. Zotero attempts to interpret the type of web page it is on, in order to draw the most useful data from it.

I find it most valuable and accurate in capturing items from library catalogs online. It also captures book data from Amazon. And if it does not see bibliographic data within the displayed website, Zotero Connector assumes that you want to capture this as a webpage, and it draws the proper bibliographic information for that.

Zotero Connector will extract the information and create a new Zotero record. The record will always be displayed in *My Library*, but it will copy a link to the record in the Zotero subcollection active at the time the connector button is pushed on the webpage.

Exercise 11: Create a Zotero record through the Zotero Connector

Let's say you need a book from the Tuscaloosa Public Library. You believe it will be of value to your research, and you are going to go ahead and put it in Zotero—primed and ready for that day when you actually get the book and take notes. Do the following:

Step 1 In Zotero, click on your *FAMILY HISTORY* collection.

Step 2 In your web browser, open the Tuscaloosa Public Library online catalog at www.tuscaloosa-library.org.

Step 3 In the search box in the top-right corner, type "Early Settlers of Pickens County" and click **Search**.

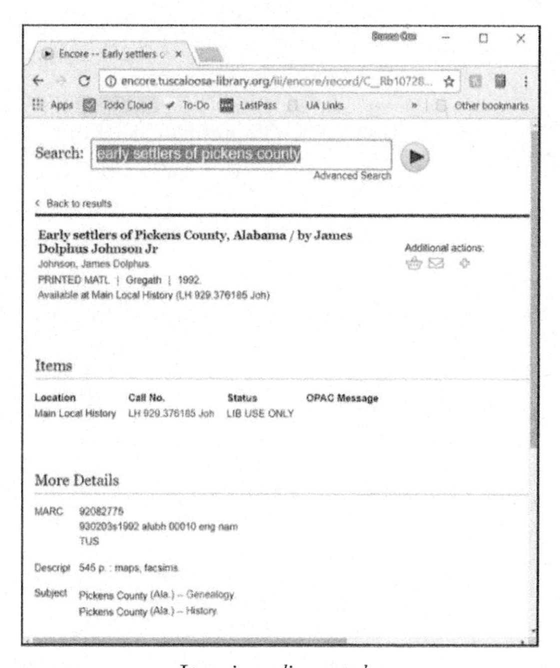

Item in online catalog

Step 4 The catalog will bring up a book by James Dolphus Johnson Jr. Click on it to display the full record. (If by chance this record is no longer in the catalog by the time of this printing, pick another book.)

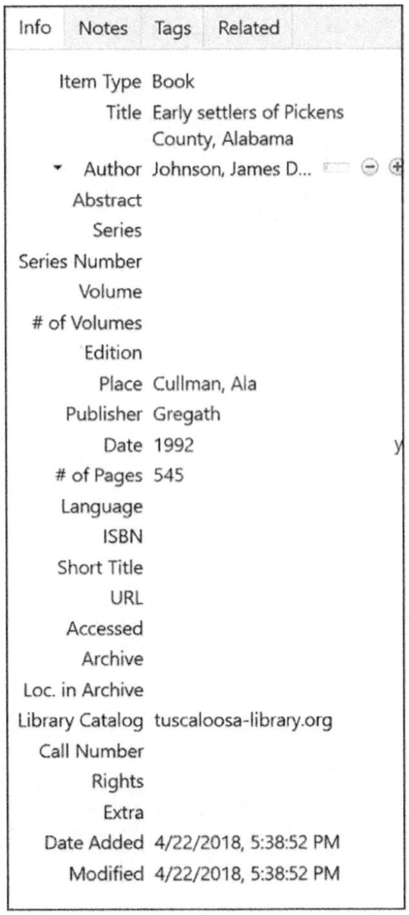

Info Notes Tags Related

Item Type	Book
Title	Early settlers of Pickens County, Alabama
Author	Johnson, James D...
Abstract	
Series	
Series Number	
Volume	
# of Volumes	
Edition	
Place	Cullman, Ala
Publisher	Gregath
Date	1992
# of Pages	545
Language	
ISBN	
Short Title	
URL	
Accessed	
Archive	
Loc. in Archive	
Library Catalog	tuscaloosa-library.org
Call Number	
Rights	
Extra	
Date Added	4/22/2018, 5:38:52 PM
Modified	4/22/2018, 5:38:52 PM

The library information has been extracted to Zotero.

Step 5 With the book record displayed on the screen, click on the Zotero Connector icon in the top right corner, which will most likely appear as a blue book. Zotero will display a message to let you know the record is being written into its database.

Step 6 Go back to Zotero. The new record should be in your *FAMILY HISTORY* collection, having pulled the record from the Tuscaloosa Public Library database.

Thanks to the wonders of "metadata," Zotero knew exactly what information to put in each field. You will always want to check behind this process because Zotero might not always have it right. Or the person who cataloged the information in the library catalog might have been inaccurate or incomplete.

Many of you will find this tool especially helpful in populating Zotero with your old research, starting with your book library. You can find the books in an online catalog and let the catalog do a lot of your work for you.

Summary

Though it is technically an "add-on," you should consider Zotero Connector an essential part of your Zotero work. It will magnify your effectiveness at research and remove the worst of the aggravation. We will cover another amazing time saver, ZotFile, next.

ZOTFILE & ADVANCED PDF MANAGEMENT 8

As you find and collect new research treasures, you will often have to set things aside to read later. You need a reading list that keeps you on top of what you have not yet done. And as you read those things, you will want to highlight passages and take notes that end up in Zotero. ZotFile allows you to create what I am calling a "reading stack" from your Zotero collection and, if needed, to transport it to your tablet or other reading device. When you get done reading, it lets you turn your notes and highlights into searchable, usable text in Zotero.

ZotFile has been designed and maintained for some years now by Joscha Legewie of New York. He charges nothing at present, only asking users to consider much-deserved donations to the continued development. He offers more complete documentation online than I will attempt here. You can find his notes at zotfile.com.

INSTALLING ZOTFILE

Do the following to install the ZotFile plug-in:

Step 1 Go to **zotfile.com** online. [Note: the instructions here are valid as of 4/22/2018. If you have problems, read the new instructions on the zotfile.com website.]

Step 2 Click **Download** from the left sidebar. A file will download to your computer.

Step 3 Go to Zotero on your desktop. From the main menu, choose **Tools—Add-ons.**

Step 4 In the Extensions view, click on the gear icon in the top-right corner. From the menu, click **Install add-on from file**.

Step 5 Browse to your Downloads folder on your computer and double-click the ZotFile program that has just been downloaded (or open the new file that is displayed at the bottom of your screen if your computer shows downloads there).

Step 6 A security window will open. Choose the **ZotFile** item in the window, then click **Install Now**.

Step 7 ZotFile will appear in the list of Extensions you have installed. Click **Restart Now** to close and reopen Zotero to activate ZotFile.

Once you have installed ZotFile, a new menu option called **ZotFile Preferences** will appear under **Tools** on your Zotero menu. You will quickly see that ZotFile offers many complex options—far more than we will attempt to cover here.

We will cover the ones I have used with the greatest value to genealogy. And we will only alter the preferences that serve those features. We will focus on ZotFile's ability to store your reading stack in a convenient way and its ability to extract your annotations (highlights and notes), creating notes in Zotero.

However, if you find that you need to investigate ZotFile's other options, in order to deal with your particular hardware configuration or file organization, you can read the add-on's documentation online at zotfile.com.

Creating a ZotFile Reading Stack

As you begin to find PDF documents you want to cite and access through Zotero, you will often be working quickly. You may find yourself at a library or archive, gathering documents rapidly that you will only have time to read with care later. Eventually, when you have some time to read, you can dig into the documents that await. ZotFile helps you to manage this, putting the PDF where you can access it, and making sure it winds up safely back in its proper place in Zotero.

ZotFile checks the PDF out of Zotero for you, much like checking out a library book. It knows what you have checked out, and ensures you know the PDF is there if you find your way back to the citation record in Zotero before you have read and returned the PDF.

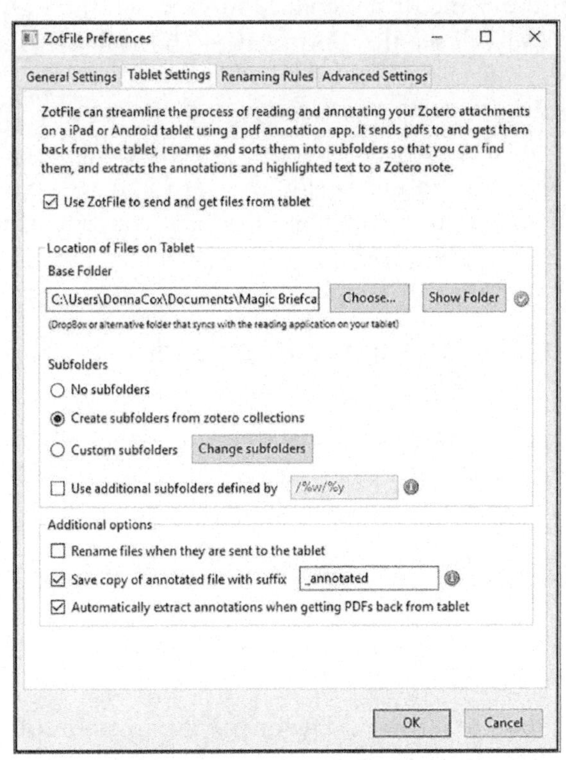

Tablet Settings tab in ZotFile Preferences

Let's begin by setting ZotFile's preferences up to create a reading stack for you to use on your laptop, tablet, or phone. Determine where you want to store your reading stack. If you have an iPad or other tablet, for example, you likely have set up a cloud folder where you can pick up and store documents you want to share between your tablet and your computer. The same could be true of reading files on your phone (though keep in mind that PDFs might not be easily readable on a phone-sized screen). If you are going to use your laptop to do your reading, and it is the same computer you use to do your Zotero work, you can pick any spot that is convenient for you on your hard drive.

To set up your ZotFile preferences, do the following:

Step 1 Open your ZotFile Preferences from your Tools menu and click on the **Tablet Settings** tab.

Step 2 In the Location of File on Table section, type the path to your reading stack folder in the Base Folder.

Step 3 Deselect **Rename files when they are sent to the tablet**. Make sure all other settings on this tab are as they appear in the diagram.

To send a PDF file from your Zotero collection to your reading stack, you will find it in your research list, right-click on it, select **Manage Attachments**, then choose to **Send to Tablet**. Zotero will put a copy of the PDF into the directory you selected in your preferences above.

Or, if you prefer, ZotFile will create a subfolder within whatever directory you established as your reading stack in the preferences. It will name the subfolder the name of the collection in which the PDF is displayed in Zotero. You will see this option at the bottom of your list of options when you right-click on the PDF.

You can use your computer's file management tool to get to your reading stack or open your ZotFile preferences to the Tablet Settings tab again and choose to **Show Folder** beside the path you set up as your storage location. If you are using a tablet or phone, you will want to link through your device to the location.

Exercise 12: Send a PDF to the reading stack

Let's experiment with the PDF we pulled into Zotero in Exercise 8 in Chapter 5. These instructions will assume you are reading the PDF on your laptop, rather than a tablet or phone, but you can use any of the options for the reading. Follow these instructions to send the PDF to your reading stack:

Step 1 In your Collections pane, click on *Zotero for Genealogy Sample Data* to display your sample research items.

Step 2 Find the research item labeled **Descriptive pamphlet of Hillsborough county, Florida**. Beneath that (you might need to expand the arrow beside the entry) you should have a PDF titled "PDFsample.pdf." Right-click on the PDF and select **Manage Attachments—Send to Tablet**.

Step 3 Open the directory you set as your Location of File on Table: Base Folder in your ZotFile Preferences. (You can go through your computer's file management system or go back to ZotFile Preferences—Tablet Settings and choose **Show Folder**.

Step 4 Open the PDF.

This is how you can create your reading stack, either reading your collected materials on your computer or accessing them through your tablet or phone. You may keep Zotero open and take notes on your reading as you go. But ZotFile offers a way to eliminate a lot of that work.

EXTRACTING ANNOTATIONS FROM PDFs

Most PDF software allows you to add comments and highlight text, if your document has recognizable text, as opposed to a graphic image. ZotFile will convert highlighted or commented text into notes.

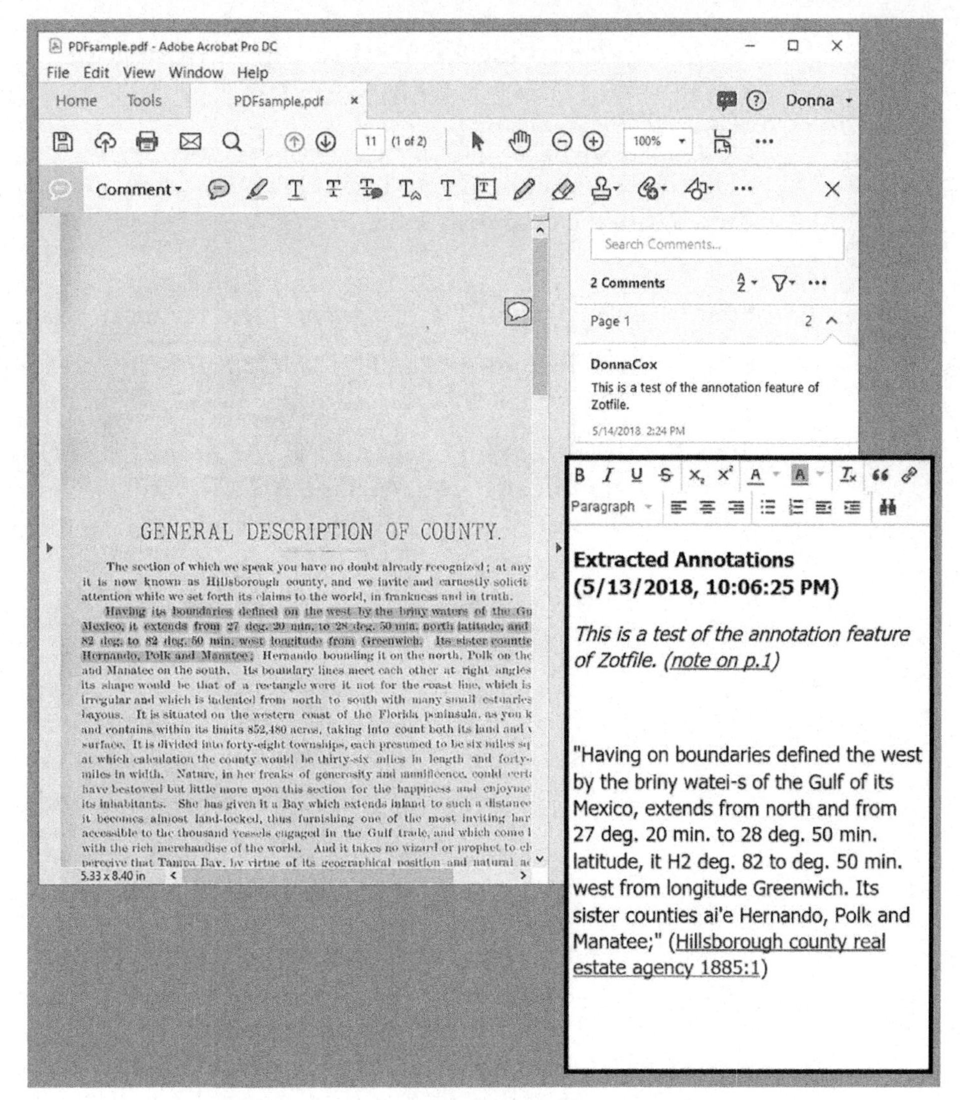

Annotations—comments and highlights—can be extracted from your PDF into your Zotero notes.

An annotated file is returned to Zotero by right-clicking on the original PDF in the Zotero research list and choosing **Manage Attachments—Get from Tablet**. If the default values were accepted in your ZotFile Preferences, ZotFile will bring the copy back into Zotero, adding the extension "_annotated" to distinguish it from the original. It will create a note called "Extracted Annotations," which contains the contents of any comments or highlighted text, identifying the page number for each.

Exercise 13: Extracting annotations from your PDF

Picking up where we left off in the last exercise, we will annotate the PDF copy sent out of Zotero by ZotFile. We will then retrieve it into Zotero with the notes extracted.

Step 1 Open your PDF file, if you closed it after the last exercise.

Step 2 Add comments and highlight selected sentences from the PDF, then close this annotated document and save it.

Step 3 In Zotero, right-click on the original PDF, called **PDF-sample**. Choose **Manage Attachments—Get from Tablet**. ZotFile will draw back into Zotero the copy of the file you have annotated, applying the text "_anno-tated" to the end of its title. Both the original and the annotated copy will remain unless you decide to get rid of one.

Step 4 ZotFile should have created a new note item under your Hillsborough County pamphlet citation. Click to open this new note titled **Extracted Annotations**. In your Details pane, you will see all of the text you highlighted or typed into comments in the PDF.

Our sample PDF in this exercise was fully embedded in Zotero—not connected externally by a link. Therefore, both copies of the PDF after this exercise are embedded in Zotero, being synced, and taking up space. On the other hand, if you had done this exercise on a PDF that resided externally and was linked into Zotero, ZotFile would treat the copy the same way—as a linked file, with the copy residing in the same directory where you put the first file.

If you prefer to keep only one copy of the PDF—the one with the annotations, you can set your ZotFile Preferences to do this.

In your preferences, go to the **Tablet Settings**. Deselect the option that says **Save copy of annotated file with suffix**. The new copy of the PDF, with your annotations, will replace the original file, carrying the same name.

Extracting annotations without sending the PDF to the stack

ZotFile will allow you to extract annotations from PDFs you have not sent to the reading stack. Right-click on the PDF in your research list, choosing **Manage Attachments—Extract Annotations**. ZotFile will create a note called "Extracted Annotations," just as it does when you send a PDF to the stack. If you are dealing with PDFs as you encounter them, rather than saving them up for later reading or processing, this method will likely be preferred.

Summary

While ZotFile is a bit more complex at the start than many Zotero features, it offers a service of great value in doing genealogical work. It also becomes quite simple to operate once you have installed it and chosen your options.

WORD PROCESSING & PAINLESS CITATIONS

9

In graduate school, I had to write numerous research papers, and finally a dissertation. The history field required we use a publishing style guide called the *Chicago Manual of Style*. I call it *CMOS* (SEE-moss), this one-thousand-plus pages of rules. Once Zotero entered the picture, though, I lost my dread of citations and bibliographies. They wrote themselves.

In genealogy, we sometimes find ourselves in need of similar help for the writing of formal articles, books, and research reports. Zotero's add-ons (interchangeably called "add-ins") for Word for Windows and LibreOffice* will take much pain out of it for anyone using standard publishing styles.

If you want to prepare research documents following the very high standards of *Evidence Explained* (*EE*) style, we will discuss that in Chapter 12. This add-on's transfer of Zotero data to your word processor will not come across in perfect *EE* format, unfortunately. But *EE* is based on *CMOS*, so you will find that Zotero gets you most of the way there, with a bit of reformatting on the back end in your word processing environment.

INSTALLING THE WORD PROCESSING ADD-ON

If you are on Zotero 5 or later, Zotero installed the necessary software when you installed or upgraded to it. For our instructional purposes

* Review Zotero's website for other possible word processor options.

here, we will use Microsoft Word for Windows as the model, but the functions should be similar for LibreOffice.

Setting up your word processing options

To properly set up this add-on, go to your Preferences and click **Cite** on the toolbar. The Style Manager offers you a list of all of the publishing styles that have been set up in Zotero. New ones are being developed continuously.

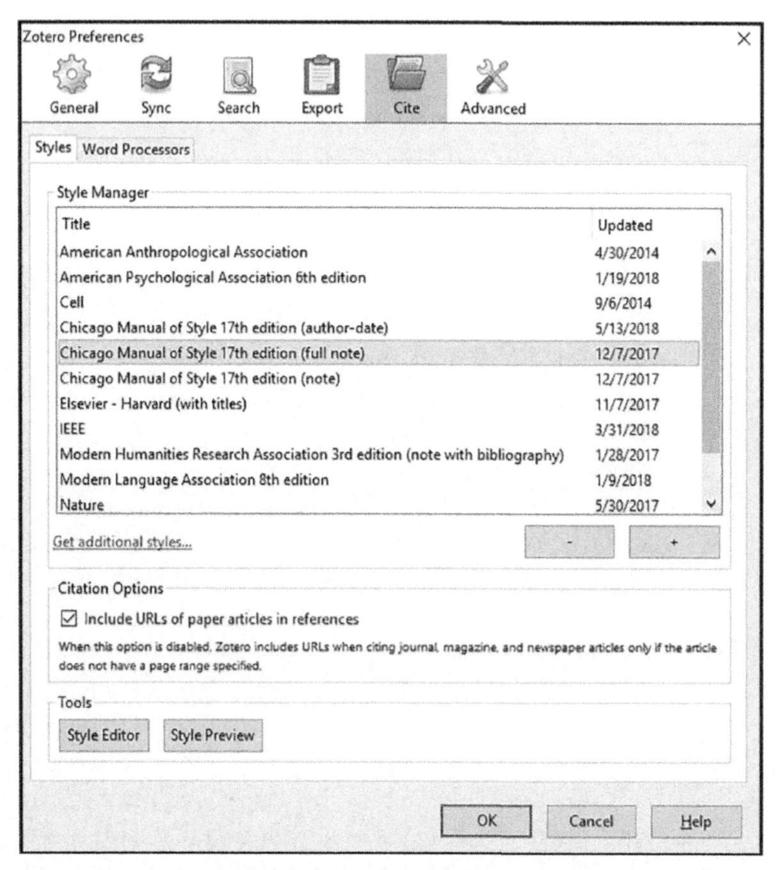

In your word processor add-on options, you select your desired style for any documents you will be creating.

Unless you have a specific style requirement other than *CMOS*, select **Chicago Manual of Style 17th edition (full note)**—or a newer version, if available. Select **Include URLs of paper articles in references**, also, unless you are writing for a publication that does not want URLs included in citations or bibliographies.

Next, check to make sure Zotero has installed the word-processor add-ons. Click on the **Word Processors** tab at the top. If it tells you that yours is not installed, click on the appropriate button. You will come back here if your word processing software ever accidentally breaks the link to Zotero and press the button to reinstall it. When everything is set up, click **OK** to save your options.

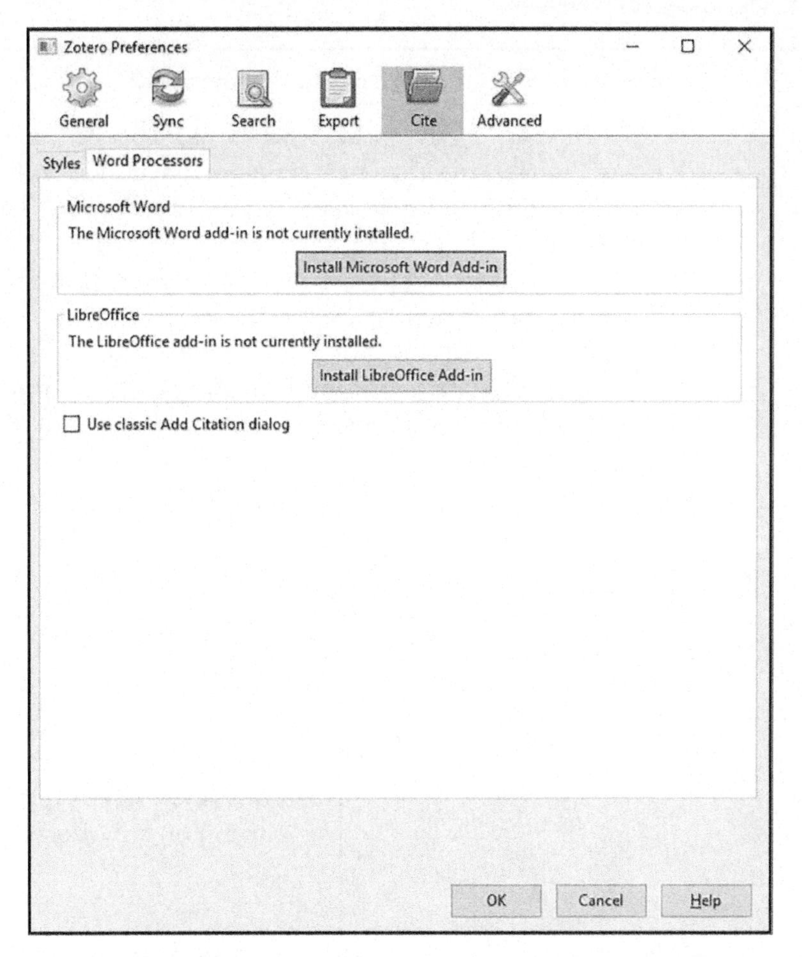

On your Preferences—Cite view, you have the option to install your word processor's add-on, if it is not already installed.

Zotero Tools in Your Word Processor

You have research stored in Zotero now and your word processing add-on set up. Now we will start using the add-on in your word processing software. Open that software, create a new blank document, and take a look at the tools Zotero has installed for you.

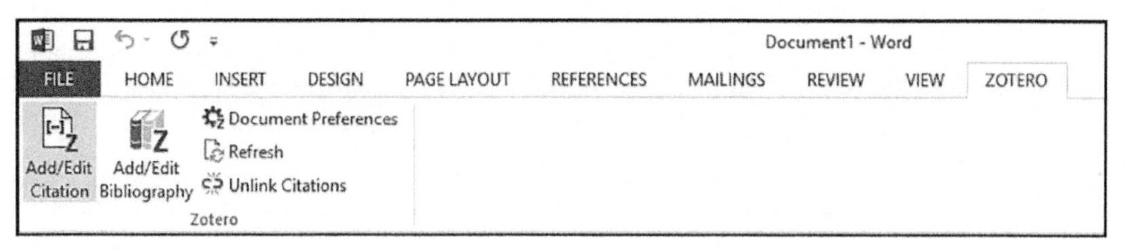

The Zotero menu option opens the tools needed to retrieve Zotero research citations.

In Word for Windows, you should see a Zotero tab on your menu bar, probably the last item, unless you have added other customizations to your software. Click on the tab, and a set of tools will appear beneath the menu bar.

With these tools, you will be able to pull citation data from Zotero and format it as footnotes or endnotes. When you have created these notes, you can then use the tools to create a bibliography. The data you pull in remains "dynamic." Let's say you find later that you had something incorrect in Zotero. You correct it in Zotero, then you can refresh your document, replacing the incorrect information throughout the entire document with your corrected Zotero information.

The Document Preferences determine how your citations will appear and behave.

Document preferences

Before you begin to work with your new document, you will want to make sure you have set your preferences. Click on **Document Preferences** on your Zotero add-on toolbar. You are offered the following options:

Citation Style

Choose one of the available publishing styles. This defaults to the one we chose in Zotero: *CMOS*.

Language

Choose the language your citations will use.

Display Citation As

Choose whether your citations are to be footnotes or endnotes. A footnote appears at the bottom of the page containing the text the note supports. An endnote appears at the end of a chapter, report, or book—gathered with all the other citations.

Store Citation as

Choose whether you want the citation to be stored as a field or a bookmark. In most cases, you will want to choose **Field**. This creates the dynamic reference in your word processor, which can be updated as information changes in Zotero. If you plan to move your document over to LibreOffice at any point, you will need to choose **Bookmark**. (Test thoroughly before transferring any document with Zotero citations to another word processing tool. Transfer a *copy*, not the original.)

Automatically update citations

Choose this if you want your document automatically to pull in changes from Zotero that would alter citations you have entered. As your document grows large, you might prefer to turn this off, to speed up your entry of new citations. If you deselect this option, you will want to click **Refresh** on the Zotero toolbar occasionally to manually update all fields in your document.

Creating Citations in Your Document

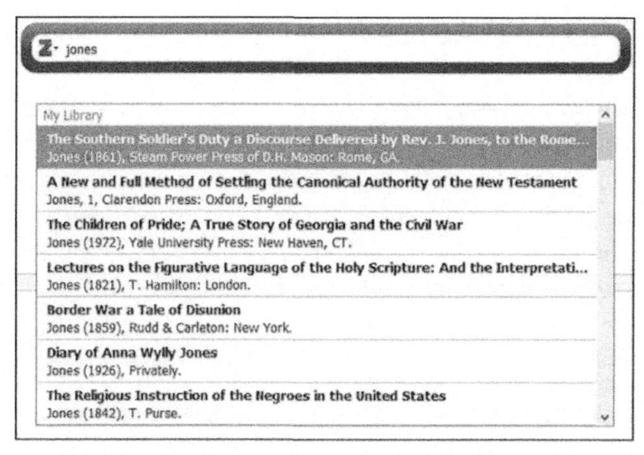

Type a string of text from your source's author or title to bring it into the drop-down list for selection.

The Zotero add-on for Word makes citation creation remarkably easy. When you have written something that requires a citation, you click the **Add/Edit Citation** icon to bring up a bar that interfaces with your Zotero database. You can find the desired Zotero record by typing in enough text to point Zotero to it. Zotero will bring up a list of all research records matching your search text. You will highlight the source record, then click **<Enter>** to create the citation. Or, just after you select the record, type in a comma and page number, to add that to the citation.

Exercise 14: Create a citation

Let's experiment with adding a citation to your empty document.

Step 1 Type this sentence into your document: "The case was decided in the late nineteenth century."

Step 2 Click on the Zotero menu option to display your tools.

Step 3 Click **Add/Edit Citation** to create your citation.

Step 4 Type "Fletcher" and select this option:

U.S. Reports: Fletcher v. Fuller, 120 U.S. 534 (1887).
United States--Supreme Court (1886), 22.

Click **<Enter>**. The Zotero add-on will insert a superscripted number at the spot where you were in the document.

[1] United States--Supreme Court, "U.S. Reports: Fletcher v. Fuller, 120 U.S. 534 (1887)," 120 US 534 Property Law § Volume 120 (1886), https://www.loc.gov/item/usrep120534/.

It will create a footnote at the bottom of your page that looks like the one above.

ADDING MULTIPLE ZOTERO CITATIONS

You will often find that you need several Zotero records to support a statement you have made in your document. To create multiple citations under a single footnote, click **Add/Edit Citations** from your Zotero menu. Type in the search string for the first record you want to cite, and select the correct one from Zotero's list. Then, rather than clicking **<Enter>**, type another search string. Repeat this until all citations are included for this one footnote.

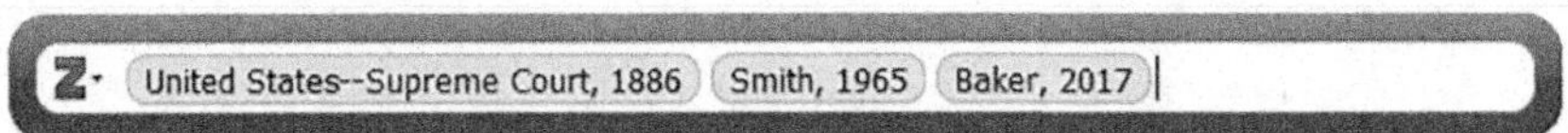

Enter multiple search strings to create a footnote with more than one citation.

Zotero will separate the citations by a semicolon, as is common practice for the *CMOS* style, looking like this:

[1] United States--Supreme Court, "U.S. Reports: Fletcher v. Fuller, 120 U.S. 534 (1887)," 120 US 534 Property Law § Volume 120 (1886), https://www.loc.gov/item/usrep120534/; Winston Smith, "Early History of Demopolis," *Alabama Review* 18, no. 3 (April 1965): 83–91; Donna Cox Baker, "The Beyond Kin Project: Documenting Enslaved Populations," *AGS Magazine* 49 (Spring/Summer 2017) (2017): 2–9.

Editing a Citation

As you create citations, you might find that you have pulled the incorrect one, or that you need to add further information to make the citation complete. Or you may realize that you had the information incorrect in Zotero to begin with. You may easily correct all of them, by one of several methods. Let's take them one by one.

Choosing a different Zotero record

If you chose the wrong Zotero record, you can do one of two things. First, you can simply delete the superscripted number in your text, which will delete the footnote or endnote. Then you go through the steps again to add a new record. Or, you can click anywhere in the footnote, and click **Add/Edit Citation** on your Zotero menu.

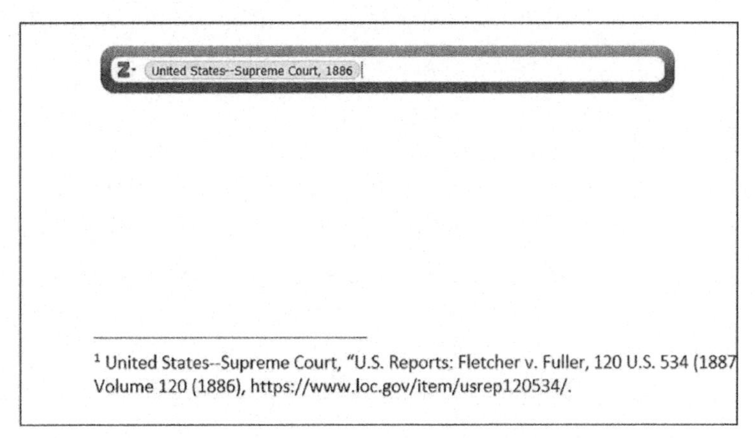

Put your cursor in the footnote and click the ***Add/Edit Citation*** *icon in your Zotero menu to edit the citation.*

The Zotero Add-on will bring up the Zotero bar again, with the selected record displayed. Backspace to remove the citation you chose, then type in text to find the one you prefer.

Adding a page number to your citation

Many of your Zotero records will contain general bibliographic information, but you will want to get more specific as you cite a specific fact you draw from the source. You will want to identify the page number, most commonly. You can add a page number as you are selecting your Zotero record, by typing a comma, a space, then your page number, and clicking the **<Enter>** key.

Type a comma and number to add a page number to your citation.

The Add-on will only accept a number after the comma. If you type letters, it will assume you want to add a second citation. When you complete your number, and press **<Enter>**, it will place the number in the appropriate page number format for your citation's style and item type.

If you decide to add a page number after you have already created the citation, click in the citation text and click the **Add/Edit Citation** button on your Zotero menu. The selection bar will reappear with your citation field displayed. Type the comma and page number after it, and Zotero will fold it into the field with a period after it. Click **<Enter>** to reformat the citation with the page number in it.

[1] United States--Supreme Court, "U.S. Reports: Fletcher v. Fuller, 120 U.S. 534 (1887)," 120 US 534 Property Law § Volume 120 (1886), 22, https://www.loc.gov/item/usrep120534/.

You may also expedite your footnote entry by typing in the search text, a comma, space, and page number *before* selecting your Zotero

Expedite your data entry with a search string and page number.

footnote. When you make your selection, the page number will be embedded.

Adding further detail to a citation

You might want to add explanatory text about your source—or further detail about how to locate the record. As long as the citation remains linked to Zotero, you can only add text at the end of the citation—*after* the Zotero-created text. If you make a change *to or within* the text that Zotero created, then attempt to do a formal edit or refresh the data, Zotero will bring up a warning message.

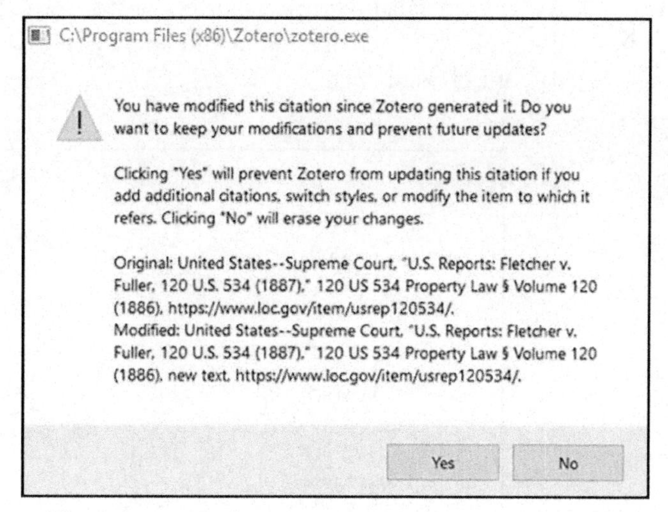

The choice to embed or alter text within a footnote or endnote that Zotero has created will render the link with Zotero invalid, if you choose to keep it.

If you choose to keep the text you have added by answering **Yes**, the connection to Zotero will be invalidated. If you make changes to this bibliographic reference within the Zotero database, it will not be updated in your document. If you answer **No**, Zotero will remove the text you have added.

To add text that can remain without invalidating the Zotero link, put your cursor behind the closing punctuation of the footnote and type there. Zotero will allow that text to remain. The bold text below demonstrates where you can add text.

[1] United States--Supreme Court, "U.S. Reports: Fletcher v. Fuller, 120 U.S. 534 (1887)," 120 US 534 Property Law § Volume 120 (1886), https://www.loc.gov/item/usrep120534/. **Here is where you may type further information for your readers.**

Keep in mind that you will not be able to insert commentary between multiple citations that have been combined into a complex footnote. You can add any desired commentary at the end of the paragraph, as you see in the bold text above.

Creating a Bibliography

Zotero's Add-on in Word offers a very simple way to create a bibliography of all sources cited within the document. Go to the spot in the document where you want the bibliography to appear. Click on the

Add/Edit Bibliography button on the Zotero toolbar, and the bibliography will be inserted at the spot. Zotero will format it according to your chosen style.

Endnotes [Compatibility Mode] - Word

FILE HOME INSERT DESIGN PAGE LAYOUT REFERENCES MAILINGS REVIEW VIEW ZOTERO Donna Cox Baker

BIBLIOGRAPHY

Alabama, Grand Lodge of. Proceedings of the Annual Communication of the Grand Lodge of Alabama Held in the City of Montgomery, Commencing December 3rd, A. D. 1883–A. L. 5883. Montgomery, AL: W. D. Brown & Co., 1884.

Arrowsmith, Aaron. "Arrowsmith South-Central United States 1817." 1:1,800,000. London, 1817. Birmingham Public Library Cartography Collection. http://bplonline.cdmhost.com/cdm/singleitem/collection/p4017coll7/id/857/rec/5.

Baker, Donna Cox. "Michael Mayberry Death Date_Research Plan," August 11, 2017. Personal Library.

Cain, Marie M., and Marilyn M. Girardi. "Big Springs Baptist Church Cemetery - Complete Survey (Randolph County AlArchives Cemeteries)." USGenWeb Archives. Accessed March 13, 2016. http://files.usgwarchives.net/al/randolph/cemeteries/bigsprng.txt.

Claiborne, J[ohn] F[rancis] H[amtramck]. Mississippi, as a Province, Territory, and State, with Biographical Notices of Eminent Citizens. Vol. I. Jackson, MS: Power & Barksdale, 1880.

Cooper, James Fenimore. The Crater; or, Vulcan's Peak. New ed. On Spine: Cooper's Novels,; 31; New York, Stringer and Townsend, 1852.

Hageness, MariLee Beatty. Ledger of Civil War Pensioners, Randolph County, Alabama. [s.l: privately published], 1996.

Jabour, Anya. "'It Will Never Do for Me to Be Married': The Life of Laura Wirt Randall, 1803-1833." Journal of the Early Republic 17, no. 2 (July 1, 1997): 193–236. http://www.jstor.org/stable/3124446.

Mackay Esq., Alex. The Western World: Travels in the United States in 1846-47. The Western World: Travels in the United States in 1846-47. London: Richard Bentley, 1850.

Swedenborg, Emanuel. Concerning the Earths in Our Solar System, Which Are Called Planets. Boston: O. Clapp, 1758yyy1839zzz.

United States--Supreme Court. U.S. Reports: Fletcher v. Fuller, 120 U.S. 534 (1887), 120 US 534 Property Law § Volume 120 (1886). https://www.loc.gov/item/usrep120534/.

PAGE 3 OF 3 522 WORDS

Zotero will create a bibliography for you at the desired spot in your document.

When you have all citations in place in your manuscript and are ready to do a final polish, you can finally choose **Unlink Citations** from the Zotero toolbar. Any editing you do to the Zotero-generated citations and bibliography will now remain intact.

SUMMARY

While this particular Zotero feature might be used only occasionally, it will be a godsend when the day comes. Even scholars who use *CMOS* or another established style regularly in their writing find the style rules oppressive to recall. This add-on allows Word and Zotero to do the recalling for you. You can concentrate on sparkling writing and worry-free genealogical research.

PART III:
APPLYING ZOTERO TO GENEALOGY

Congratulations on having gotten through all of the introductory material. Now we get to the most essential thing you came here for: Zotero as applied to genealogy. As I am sure you realize, there will never be a comprehensive book on a subject like this. There are simply too many variables in genealogy. But the essential elements are here—the beginnings upon which you can build.

ORGANIZING YOUR FILING SYSTEM 10

Filing systems are very personal things. I have watched many a genealogy lecture with yet another system and wondered, "What were they thinking?" Honestly, I find most of them needlessly complex. But here's the beauty of it. It's up to you. What works for you?

THE MAIN THING: ONE SYSTEM FOR ALL

Organizing your Zotero system successfully depends on following this one rule: mimic the filing system you use outside of Zotero. If you have found that a complex alphanumeric coding system that identifies each ancestor, surname, and type of file is your cup of tea, then mimic it here.

If you do not yet have an established organizational system for your genealogy records or are unsatisfied with what you have, I will encourage you to try the very simple system I use. I describe it below, in case it is of use.

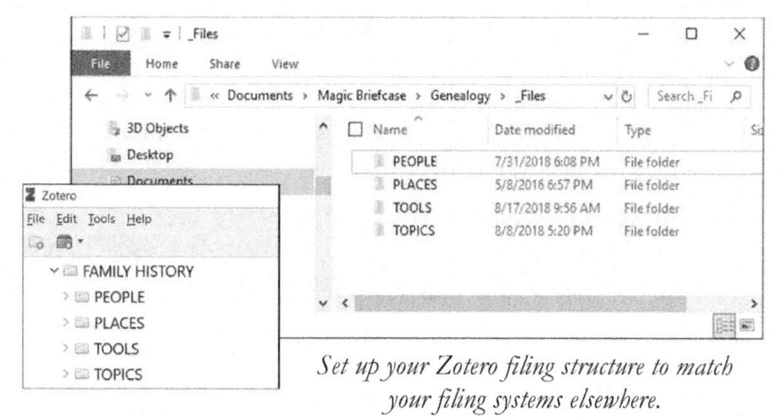

Set up your Zotero filing structure to match your filing systems elsewhere.

Just do yourself the favor of applying the same filing system every place you are filing materials, if possible. Apply it in Zotero, on your computer hard drive, and in your paper files (if you continue to keep paper). You might not have control over source organization in your online tree software, where you are tying your research to very specific facts. But keep the rest of it consistent, and you will minimize your research troubles.

MY VERY SIMPLE FILING SYSTEM

The system I use blends ideas I have picked up from others, combined with my own "tweaks" as I sought to find places for things. No doubt, my system will be tweaked again in the future, as needed. That is the beauty of going simple.

Just about everything I might need to file related to my family history work can be categorized as one of the following:

- PEOPLE
- PLACES
- TOOLS
- TOPICS

Organizing people

I organize people first by surname, then by given name with birth and death years, if known. Surname variants can be included in the label, like "Cox/Coxe." If the variants create confusion in alphabetical order, say "Cox/Koch," you can use the variants, then create an empty folder labeled, "Koch (see Cox)."

I place women in the families of their birth, when known, since it is likely to be the most stable surname. If I only know a woman's given name and her attachment to her husband's family, I place

PEOPLE
- Avery
- Baker
- Barsh
- Bennett
- Brooks
- Burson
  - _General Burson Resources
  - HS Burson
  - Jackson Jasper Burson (1872 - 1951)
  - James C. Burson (1837 - 1910)
  - Rebecca A Burson
  - Tobitha Jane Burson (1893/4 - 1922)
- Carnathan

People are organized by their birth surname, then their given name and birth and death years.

her temporarily in a folder inside her husband's folder. I label it something like, "Penelope wife of John (1821 -)." When I find her maiden name, she will be moved to her birth family's surname.

Keep in mind that changing a folder label will break Zotero's link to the attachments within the folder. So when you discover the missing birth year or move the woman to her birth family's folder, know that you must reconnect any broken attachments in the folder. The good news is this: since you are using the same file structure everywhere you are filing information, you can easily find the material where you stored it on your hard drive. Simply click on any broken attachments, and click **Locate**, then find the new location.

When I find a document that names many different family members within a surname, I create a folder on my hard drive called "_General [Surname] Resources," rather than make multiple copies of the attachment. It exists only once on my hard drive. Meanwhile, all of the people named in it have a link to that same document created in Zotero.

Also, some documents will name multiple surnames I am researching. On my hard drive, above the surnames, I have a file labeled "_Multifamily Resources." I store such documents there and, again, link all applicable people in my Zotero files to the one document.

The most important thing, as you label your PEOPLE folders, is to make sure you distinguish similar names. You might want to add a county or some other distinguishing word, like "doctor" or "preacher," for people with the same name. Choose the thing that will help you to know on sight which Tom Smith folder is the one you want to use.

If you think your surname folders will get too voluminous, you can add an organizational layer above them—working you and your spouse's branches separately, for example. Or if you do research for other people, you will almost certainly want to separate their research from your own.

Whatever you choose, though, keep the rules to a minimum, the complexities absent. Create a system you can maintain and that your heirs will understand.

Places

For resources about a locality, I store materials in my PLACES folder. Most of my work at this stage is in the United States, and will likely always be the major research area. So I organize my U.S. locations directly under PLACES, without forcing another layer above them called "United States." For other nations I am researching, I work within a

Organize places by major political entities, with smaller subsets nested inside. States hold counties, which hold cities, which hold institutions.

subfolder of PLACES labeled "_International." The underscore at the beginning of the label forces it to the top of the sorted folders.

In dealing with U.S. localities, I organize first by state, then county, then city. If you wish to, you can go even more specific, with a folder for a church or cemetery or school within the locality. I only go to this level of detail when I have a number of resources about a single institution.

Places, like women's names, can change names, boundaries, and even sovereigns over time. Do not stress too much about how to organize these bouncing details. Just make sure you leave yourself a breadcrumb trail. Let's say you have chosen to store a document under its name at the time the document was created: "New Merkle." When you are looking for that document ten years from now, you might think you stored it in the name of the locality now, "Cahaba Heights." You can choose to name the two folders "New Merkle (now Cahaba Heights)" and "Cahaba Heights (formerly New Merkle)," if you think that would be helpful. Or you can put both names in the notes for the document so that a search helps you find it. Or, you might choose to create a note within the locality folder that gives some of its history—creating the needed breadcrumb trail in that document.

Tools

In the TOOLS folder I collect information about tools that will help me in my research. Zotero is such a tool, and I want to grab articles that teach me how to use it optimally. I can store software instructions here and warranties, receipts, and correspondence of value.

I also keep wish lists here, when I have an idea how a tool developer might improve the product. I can write up my "hacks" and workarounds to the product's limitations. I can make note of reported bugs, and store notices of what is supposed to be added to future versions of the product.

It is especially helpful for the evaluation of tools I do not yet have. I can collect articles and surveys that give me the perspective of others on one product category or another.

Topics

In genealogy, I find myself researching all sorts of topics like the laws regarding unwed mothers in 1850s Heard County, Georgia, or the influenza epidemic of 1919 in Birmingham, Alabama. I might open the newsletter of a local genealogy society and see a great article I want to save, about ICD codes on death certificates. I will want to consult that again, so I drop it into a TOPICS folder called "Death certificates."

I might want to write a blog post about how to determine what the weather was like in a particular place and time. I will drop relevant notes into a folder called "Weather," until I have a sufficient amount to write a meaningful post.

Summary

You can be confident that you will encounter exceptions to every rule you create for yourself in your filing system. Rather than seeking a perfect system, which will fail you, make sure you leave yourself clues to find your way back to any document. Your Zotero search capabilities can find things in the most obscure places, so long as you have left a few keywords in your record that you will remember.

As you begin to create records in Zotero, the filing system will get simpler with use. A complexity arises when a particular source has information on many things related to your research—a census record, for example. Is it one source or many? We address that next.

11 One Source Record or Many: A Choice

As you prepare to capture your research information and citations, you will be faced with choices. A single major source might contain information about a thousand people in your family tree. Would you make the major source a single Zotero research entry, or would each record about an ancestor within that major source become its own record? You can do either or both. The important thing is to think about what you need to be able to draw from Zotero. Pick the most efficient method for your needs in any given case.

A Source Record with Many Notes

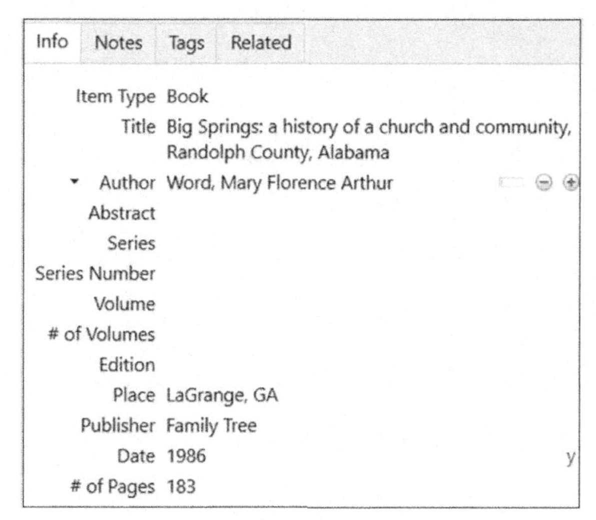

A single published book might hold many references to family members in multiple branches of your family.

A very typical source in your genealogy might be a local history of a place your ancestors lived. If it is a small town and your ancestors in multiple family lines lived there for many generations, you will likely find family on many pages in the book. There are a number of ways to document such a situation in Zotero.

Certainly, you will want a traditional bibliographic entry for the published book—one place where you document it as a whole. But you have a decision to make about handling all of the references to your family. If you want to capture a single bibliographic reference for a book, as entered in the image above, the formatted citation would appear like this:

Word, Mary Florence Arthur. *Big Springs: A History of a Church and Community, Randolph County, Alabama*. LaGrange, GA: Family Tree, 1986.

All notes under one reference

The most basic way to handle this situation is to create the book reference (or website or other major source) only once in Zotero and have all of the notes beneath it. If the major source mentions multiple branches of your family, you could create a note per surname. If you are citing references in a book, be certain you include the page number, so that you can easily find the reference again, and so that you can cite the source in published citations.

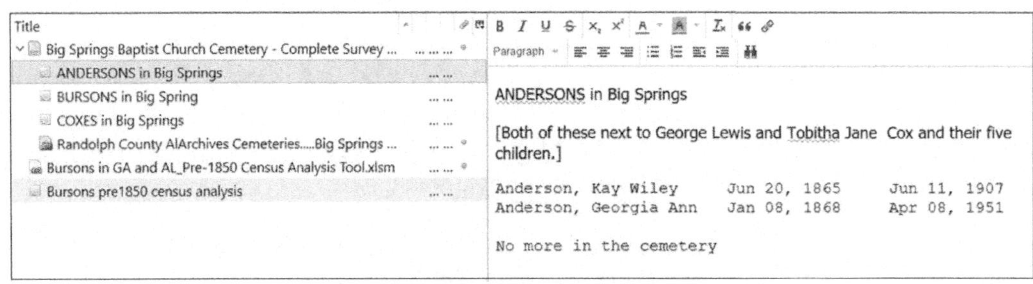

This website contains burial information for three different family surnames of interest. A separate note is created for each surname.

Using book sections for finer detail

You might find it useful to break up the notes or your citations into finer detail. Perhaps a single note per surname has become too bulky.

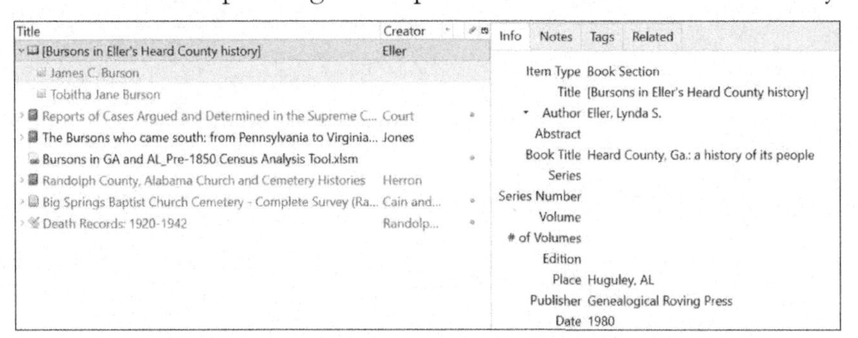

A "book section" reference type can be used to segment bulky references in a single source, in this case segmenting by surname.

Or, maybe you want to create separate notes per person. You can create Zotero references with the Book Section item type and create section titles like "[Bursons in Eller's Heard County history]." There is no chapter in Lynda Eller's book that is about the Burson family, but I can create this citation and collect everything she mentions about Bursons in the book.

The notes added to this reference can be labeled by ancestor—collecting information about each separately. You will still have the full book citation information but will have a copy per surname.

As another example, the entire book might be about a single surname in your family. Each chapter is about a generation. You might want to create multiple Zotero references as "book sections," chapter by chapter rather than (or in addition to) the full book. The title of the chapter becomes the book section title. You can then break up your notes by generation, and your notes might be about specific children in that generation.

A local history book might include a labeled section about one or several of your family branches. Or it might include a biography section about a specific ancestor. You could use a book section to deal with this piece of the main source separately.

When using book sections, the section title becomes the title that displays in your Research List pane. If you create a bibliographic reference, it includes the section title. A book section labeled "Caswell" in Lynda Eller's history of Heard County, Georgia, appears like this:

Eller, Lynda S. "Caswell." In *Heard County, Ga.: A History of Its People*, 173. Huguley, AL: Genealogical Roving Press, 1980.

This works well for formally labeled book sections, like "Caswell" above. If you are using a book section as an informal way of breaking up a large mass of information, though—as in the example of "[Bursons in Eller's Heard County history]" above—you would not use the section title in a formal bibliographic reference. You will be reminded to pull it out when you see the reference looking like this:

Eller, Lynda S. "[Bursons in Eller's Heard County history]." In *Heard County, Ga.: A History of Its People*, 173. Huguley, AL: Genealogical Roving Press, 1980.

A CASE STUDY

There will be occasions in which you will find it useful to make a separate bibliographic entry for a number of items that you might have incorporated under a single citation. While you could create a single entry for a newspaper, for example, then put the date and title of the articles in your notes, it can be useful to make each newspaper article its own entry. The newsletter articles, being dated, can create a timeline of events.

My first experiment with the Newspapers.com database brought delightful results. A search for my 2nd-great-grandfather Jacob Mayberry's name brought 110 hits in Alabama newspapers. He was the county sheriff of Choctaw County, and the town apparently took note every time his daughters held a party. They reported it the night his wife accidentally set the house on fire while cooking dinner. These are great nuggets of family life, and I am lucky to have them.

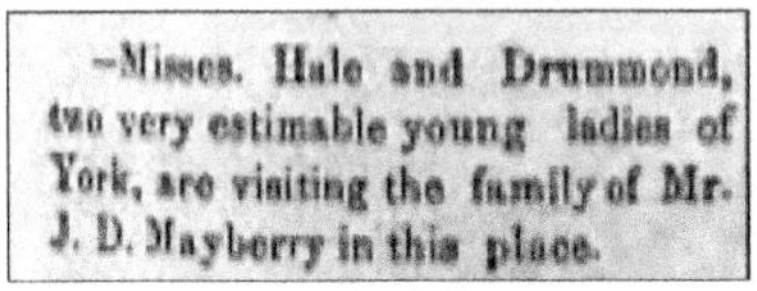

—Misses. Hale and Drummond, two very estimable young ladies of York, are visiting the family of Mr. J. D. Mayberry in this place.

Choctaw Herald *July 24, 1890.*

His name also appeared in the paper, though, every time property was seized and every time they listed the "County Directory" of local officials. Many of these articles have little to offer me in their specifics. Still, rather than cite the name of the newspaper only once in Zotero, I chose to make each article its own entry in Zotero. By creating them in Zotero separately, I am creating a timeline of my ancestor's activities over nearly five decades. I know where he was and what counties were choosing to report on him at any given time.

Title	Date	Publication
Announcements [Party of youngsters at home of JD May...	1890-04-03	Choctaw Herald
Minutes of the Democratic Convention, held at Butler, C...	1890-05-29	Choctaw Herald
County Directory	1890-07-23	Choctaw Advocate
Notice. [Visit of Misses Hale and Drummond]	1890-07-24	Choctaw Herald
County Directory	1890-08-20	Choctaw Advocate
Commissioner's Court	1890-08-27	Choctaw Advocate
Gaining Ground	1890-08-27	Choctaw Advocate
County Directory	1890-09-03	Choctaw Advocate
County Convention	1890-09-04	Choctaw Herald
[n.t.--J.D. Mayberry and State Alliance]	1890-10-16	Choctaw Herald

Dated articles can create a timeline of a family's whereabouts and activities.

TESTING YOUR BIBLIOGRAPHIC DATA—STYLE PREVIEW

Much of your work to document sources will be experimental in the beginning. There will be many records that do not fit established models, and you will need to document them as well as possible. Follow this procedure to see how your citation will look as you make various changes to your Zotero entry:

Step 1 Size your Zotero workspace to cover only half of your monitor.

Step 2 Find and click on your record in the Research List.

Step 3 From the Main Menu, choose **Edit—Preferences**, and click on the **Cite** button.

Step 4 Be sure the **Styles** tab is selected. In the Style Manager, click on **Chicago Manual of Style 17th edition (full note)** and click the **Style Preview** button near the bottom of your window.

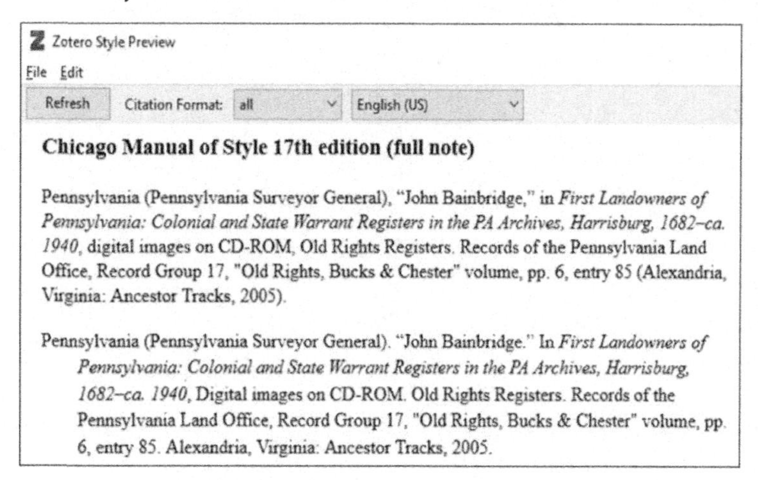

The Zotero Style Preview shows you what your record will look like when formatted as a footnote or bibliographic reference.

Step 5 Position the new window so that it is visible beside your Zotero main window. Click **Refresh** to bring your record's bibliographic formats into view. Scroll to show the *CMOS* formats.

Step 6 If the style is not satisfactory to your needs—something is missing or will be confusing in retrospect—make adjustments to your Zotero record.

Step 7 Refresh the format window and review it again. Keep doing this until you have the format that will work best for you.

SUMMARY

You may use a number of different strategies for dealing with a bulk of research findings within a single major source. In any given case, you need to ask yourself how you will find the information again. If you plan to extract citations from Zotero for use in published materials, ask yourself how the method you have chosen will work. You will want to minimize duplication of effort without losing benefits later in your projects.

The amount of time you are willing to spend on citations will depend in no small part on whether you plan to formally publish your work. If you do have that future in mind, you will want to know how to use Zotero to capture the information recommended by the *Evidence Explained* standard. We cover that next.

WORKING WITH EVIDENCE EXPLAINED 12

Proper and adequate source citations present one of the greatest challenges to those trying to do genealogy with excellence. We cannot ask anyone to trust our "facts" without highly credible and, ideally, *verifiable* sources. Variations of genealogical citation style have emerged over the decades, and family tree software developers have attempted with varying degrees of success to mesh citation style with online tree development. While it is safe to say that no one has been able to make excellent genealogical citations easy yet, we can make it workable by blending the thorough intelligence of Elizabeth Shown Mills's *Evidence Explained: Citing History Sources from Artifacts to Cyberspace* (*EE*) with the functionality of Zotero.

EVIDENCE EXPLAINED AND THE MISSION OF CITATIONS

Thoroughly vetted and generally accepted as the style of choice by the genealogy field, *EE* establishes a robust standard for citing sources. It establishes the information needed to identify our information's sources and chain of evidence adequately. It amplifies the standards of the history field, encompassing much that has been lacking for history and is absolutely essential for genealogical research.

Mills asserts that historical citation is an art rather than a science, and I wholeheartedly agree. (*EE*, 41) The records of the human past have been created by people of vastly different cultures, educations, and technologies. There can be no one-size-fits-all format that will handle all of our sources of information. As we create citations, the most important questions we need to ask are these:

- Can this citation lead people back to this specific source, if it is accessible?
- Does this citation demonstrate that a reliable source has been used as evidence?

These questions represent the mission of a citation. The style rules might not always fit a particular source. And the style rules and the citation software might not always play well together. But the art comes in creating the outcome that best serves the *mission.*

ZOTERO AND *EE* IN COOPERATION

Zotero has been engineered to work with the established citation standards of most of the scholarly world, but even this powerhouse struggles a bit with the expanded standards of *EE*. Any desire to draw perfectly formed *EE* style from Zotero (or any other software I have tried) will come up short at times. Dr. Mills designed the unprecedentedly thorough *EE* style to meet the mission of excellent citations, not to confine itself to database best practices. So we improvise, where needed.

EE names many "elements" you will not find in Zotero by the same labels, if they exist at all. *EE*'s helpful "QuickCheck Models" illustrate its elements—the bolded and underlined labels above the citation data in the image below. Zotero has no element labeled "Jurisdiction/Agency," for example, and "Item Type" means something completely different than it means in Zotero. In Zotero, a "Repository" is called an "Archive." You will want to look past labels to functions.

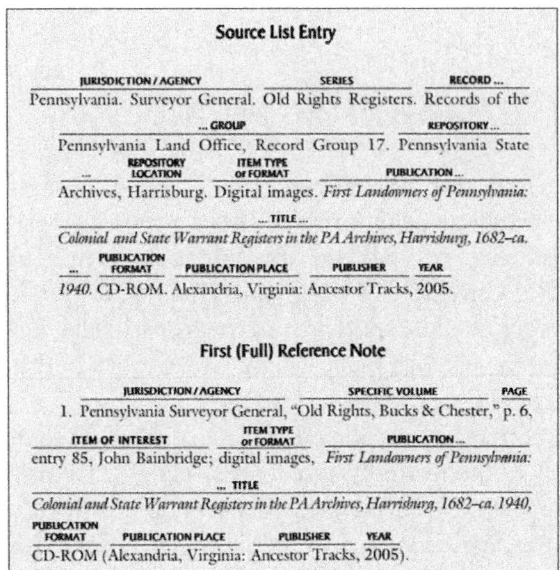

Source List Entry

JURISDICTION / AGENCY — SERIES — RECORD ...
Pennsylvania. Surveyor General. Old Rights Registers. Records of the
... GROUP — REPOSITORY ...
Pennsylvania Land Office, Record Group 17. Pennsylvania State
... — REPOSITORY LOCATION — ITEM TYPE OF FORMAT — PUBLICATION ...
Archives, Harrisburg. Digital images. *First Landowners of Pennsylvania:*
... TITLE ...
Colonial and State Warrant Registers in the PA Archives, Harrisburg, 1682–ca.
... — PUBLICATION FORMAT — PUBLICATION PLACE — PUBLISHER — YEAR
1940. CD-ROM. Alexandria, Virginia: Ancestor Tracks, 2005.

First (Full) Reference Note

JURISDICTION / AGENCY — SPECIFIC VOLUME — PAGE
1. Pennsylvania Surveyor General, "Old Rights, Bucks & Chester," p. 6,
ITEM OF INTEREST — ITEM TYPE OF FORMAT — PUBLICATION ...
entry 85, John Bainbridge; digital images, *First Landowners of Pennsylvania:*
... TITLE
Colonial and State Warrant Registers in the PA Archives, Harrisburg, 1682–ca. 1940,
PUBLICATION FORMAT — PUBLICATION PLACE — PUBLISHER — YEAR
CD-ROM (Alexandria, Virginia: Ancestor Tracks, 2005).

QuickCheck Model from Evidence Explained*, p. 492*

Our goal is to get everything *EE* considers essential into a functional place in Zotero. Once you look at the elements *functionally*, rather than seeking a *literal* match in Zotero, you will find that Zotero can handle your *EE* data. And, with only a few exceptions, it will automate the creation of quite worthy, if not perfect, footnotes, endnotes, or bibliographic entries. Sometimes, you will paste several *EE* elements together in a single Zotero field, as you see in the image below. Sometimes, you will use a Zotero field creatively—putting something there that Zotero did not initially intend but will handle adequately. And once in a while you might create a free-form *EE* citation in a Zotero note. You will find a place for everything.

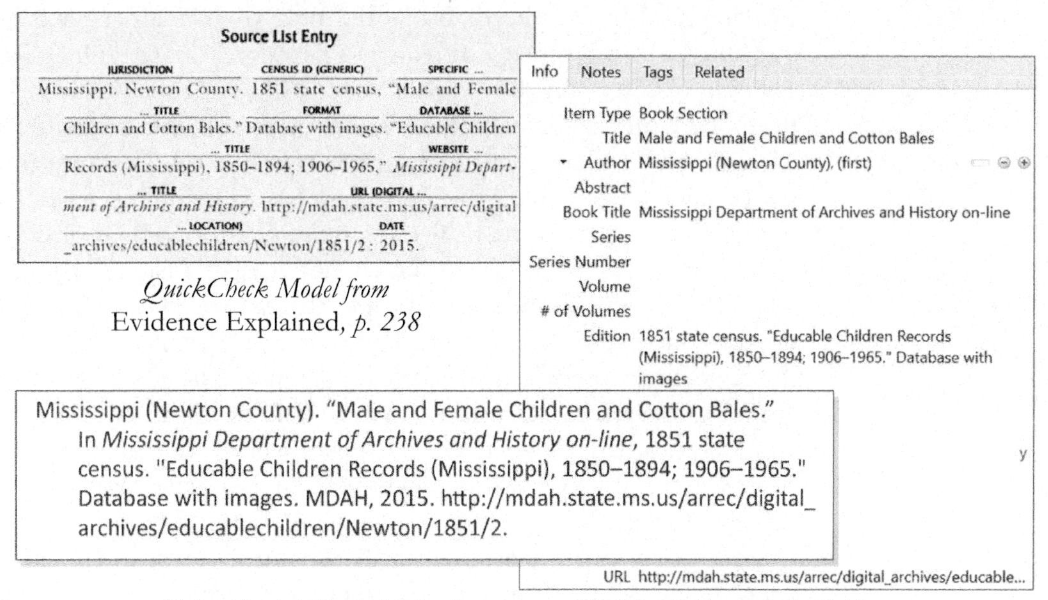

QuickCheck Model from Evidence Explained, *p. 238*

Using Zotero's Book Section item type and Edition field creatively (right), EE's bibliographic format (above) becomes the citation below.

While Zotero creates an efficient framework for data—seeking repeatable and efficient patterns, as databases must—*EE* addresses an unwieldy breadth of sources. Genealogical research includes virtually any object or body of information that might shed light on a human life, including DNA. So, we have to get a bit creative now and then to fit an *EE* square peg into Zotero's round hole. In the example above, three *EE* elements have been gathered in the Edition field in Zotero. And while the resulting bibliographic entry is not a perfect match to the *EE* version, it is remarkably close and artfully serves the mission.

To make this art and mission successful, you must ensure that, while a resource is in your hands, you capture into Zotero all you will need to meet *EE* standards. Just know, before you begin, that some citations will need a human polishing to get *EE*-perfected format, if your publisher requires it. Some publishers will be fine with the artistic license you are taking through Zotero-generated format, so long as you are generating consistent citations throughout your publication that serve the citation mission and meet *EE*'s content standards.

MAXIMIZING *EE*-TO-ZOTERO CONVERSIONS

At nearly 900 pages in length, no one expects you to master *EE*—carrying it all in your head. While the bulk of *EE* is designed to be consulted as a reference, not read as a narrative, do carefully read the opening chapters on the "Fundamentals of Evidence Analysis" and the "Fundamentals of Citation." Here, Mills explains brilliantly why citations and evidence standards matter. Only as you get familiar with the genuine goals behind the *EE* standards will you know when and how you can exercise artistic license in the *EE*-to-Zotero conversion.

At nearly 900 pages, also, you will not want to carry the paper version of *EE* with you on research trips. Still, you need it on hand at the time you are gathering research. Therefore, I recommend that you get the Kindle version of *EE* and have it on your device whenever you are gathering or processing research. As you are keying data into Zotero, you will want to know what *EE* expects you to document about the source. Do not leave a source behind until you have captured everything you need.

Zotero functions very well for those citing sources in *Chicago Manual of Style (CMOS)* format. *CMOS* tends to be the style of choice for most scholarly publishers and is the standard style in the field of history. *EE* was built on the *CMOS* base, and to the degree that the two styles agree, Zotero serves both. *EE* expands substantially over *CMOS*, though, and the expansions require the creative use of Zotero.

The *EE* expansion lies predominantly in two areas. First, *EE* deals with types of evidence that are rarely addressed by other style guides. It deals with artifacts, like tombstones, embroidered samplers, and medals. It recognizes the significance of maiden names, personal knowledge, and local lore. And it deals with the vital importance of citing negative evidence—evidence that something was not found.

The second expansion of *EE* deals with the problems of derivative copies of sources. *EE* suggests you cite the original creator of the material (if known), the provider of the version you are using, and any middle agents between the two. (*EE*, 47–48) If your source is the derivative of a derivative of an original, then you have three layers of citation in your chain of evidence. You are acknowledging anything that might have altered the new iteration in transit. You are acknowledging that you did not see the original, but a copy of a copy—letting your reader decide if your source is trustworthy.

These expansions place heavier expectations on Zotero than *CMOS* and other citation styles do. Read the sections below to learn the tricks for getting what you need from Zotero, while honoring *EE*'s standards.

Using what Zotero offers

If you have been following the exercises in this manual, you have Zotero set up to use *CMOS* as its foundation. Given its common core with *EE*, much of Zotero can work as designed to create *EE*-compatible citations. Always begin by looking for a Zotero item type that is already a match to *EE*.

Most published materials will be cited similarly in *EE* and *CMOS*. Zotero's formats will usually give you what you need to cover all of the elements *EE* suggests for basic manuscripts, letters, interviews, legal cases, artwork, and other common source types.

When *EE* recommends a type of citation that Zotero does not offer, begin by locating the Zotero format that is best able to contain the data you want to capture. In Chapter 2, in the section titled "Retrieving sample data for Zotero for Genealogy," you copied from your Group Library a collection labeled *Zotero Bibliographic Formats*. If you are not finding this in your Zotero workspace, return to Chapter 2 and retrieve the sample data.

Every field has been populated with placeholder data. Use the Style Preview to see Zotero formats for each item type.

Zotero Bibliographic Formats contains an entry for each available Zotero item type format, with placeholder text in each field that describes the field. Use the section titled "Testing your bibliographic data—Style Preview," discussed in the previous chapter, to see how Zotero formats the data entered in each field.

This is important because some of Zotero's fields are for storage only and are not included in the formatting of a bibliographic entry. Be sure you choose what you need based on the citation *output*, rather than the data input.

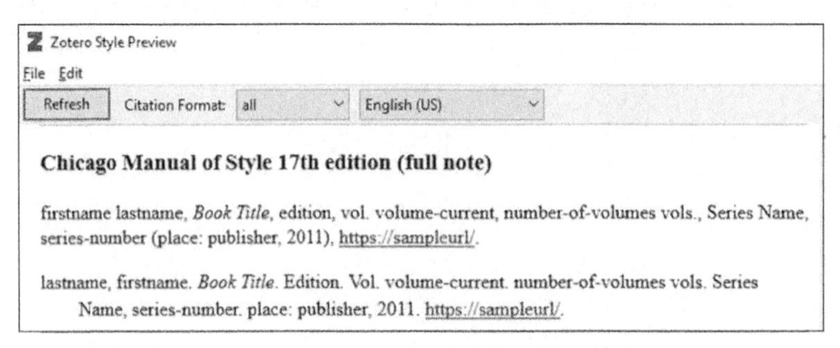

Use the Style Preview to examine how Zotero placed the sample data. Find a format that appears capable of creating your desired EE format.

To the degree possible, make a logical decision about which *EE* citation material belongs where. The Author field in Zotero will usually be where you want to put the person who created the source at hand. The Archive field will reflect where the material you consulted is held. The Publisher can be the entity who disseminated the source. Sometimes the match between *EE* elements and Zotero fields is obvious. If it is not, look at *EE*'s sample citations and figure out how to configure its elements to end up in the place you want them in a Zotero citation.

In the Style Preview, examine how Zotero used the placeholder text in any given item type. The image above shows the reference note and bibliographic entry for the Book item type. You will notice several ways that Zotero has altered the placeholder text.

The book title has been converted to title case and italicized. The abbreviation "vol." has been inserted in front of the volume number, and the abbreviation "vols." has been inserted after the number of volumes. The series title has been converted to title case. (Zotero will also strip out quotation marks put around text in the Series and Series Number fields.)

You will also notice that many fields that were populated in the Zotero record do not appear in the citations. These fields are to store extra information that is valuable to your work. There will be a few occasions in which you might want to store data in one of these fields for later embedding in a citation. See the section below titled "Method 1: Zotero format with derivatives in Extra field" for details. But in most cases, you will only want to put citation material in the fields that Zotero uses in its creation of the citation text.

Get to know how Zotero formats these fields, and it will become easy to figure out which item type will best mimic an *EE* style format. I encourage you to look particularly at the formats for emails, interviews, letters, and presentations. Zotero's citation format will be incorporating the text you entered in special ways. In the Presentation item type, for example, you will enter a Type, like "Speech." And you will enter a Meeting Name like "Southern Historical Association Annual Meeting." Zotero will reformat it to say, "Speech presented at the Southern Historical Association Annual Meeting."

I also recommend you create a cross-reference between your Kindle version of *EE* and your Zotero data to eliminate work in the future. When I put a new entry in Zotero based on information in *EE,* I put "EE" and the page number in the Extra field in Zotero. As I perfect my references before publication, I will easily find the discussion in *EE* that supports this specific entry. Also, whenever I have successfully converted an *EE* model reference to Zotero form, I add a note in my Kindle version of *EE*, identifying what item type I used in Zotero and any special handling I did to perfect the footnote. Any time I have the need to use that particular *EE* format again, I will know exactly what to do.

WORKING AROUND THE CHALLENGES

While Zotero will likely handle your *EE* requirements better than most citation managers for "Big-R Research," you will still face challenges. The notes in this section describe how I am working around these hurdles. You will likely be creating your own workarounds as we all go forward.

Reference note v. bibliography complexities

CMOS has long engaged in what is, to me, an exercise in frustration by altering things only slightly between the reference note and the bibliography. For example, the reference note puts a person's name in [first name] [last name] format. The bibliography puts it in [last name], [first name] form. *CMOS* and *EE* both tend to put some elements in lower case, separated by commas, in the reference note. But in the bibliography, the same text must be in sentence case, separated by periods.

While I am told this is done for good reason, I still hope for a better way someday.

These frustrations are amplified somewhat by *EE*, due to its many elements. Zotero does its best to take care of this note-to-bibliography conversion for standard *CMOS* items, but it is not geared to handle the "hacks" we are using—putting multiple *EE* items in a single Zotero field. If your publisher is a purist on *EE* style, you will have to do some clean-up of these things once you have created your notes and bibliography in a document for publication.

Short (subsequent) citation complexities

Once you have thoroughly cited a source, *CMOS* allows subsequent references to be a more sparing reference, often cutting it down to an author's last name, the book title, and a page number. You can even cut the subtitle from the book's title or shorten it to a few defining words. Zotero can handle this for *CMOS*-style references, cutting the title down to whatever you put in its Short Title field.

EE's general guidelines for the shorter citations can be found in section 2.45 on page 65, and more detailed counsel is found in the various chapters. It tends in some cases to be a bit more "surgical" in its shortening than Zotero can manage. For example, it counsels you to abbreviate references to places, in the second reference. Therefore, your first reference might call a place "Jefferson County, Alabama," but the shortened reference will be "Jefferson Co., Ala." The choice about which elements in the *EE* reference need to be repeated in the short reference depends on the nature of the source.

This one-by-one surgical shrinking will reduce the bulk of footnotes in a publication, as intended. But this limits any hope of automating your shortened references, using the Zotero's word processing add-on.

I recommend you shorten titles where you can in the Short Title field. Let Zotero create the second references as it will in your document, using the Word add-on. Then go back through before publication to ensure second references meet *EE* standards—and your own preferences. Ask yourself if readers will have trouble connecting the subsequent reference to its bibliographic entry. If they will, rework it before you publish it.

Author as Jurisdiction

The creator of many of your sources will be a local jurisdiction, often a county or city within a state or country. *EE* suggests that jurisdictions take on different formats for use in the footnotes versus the bibliography. "Jefferson County, Alabama" needs to be flipped to "Alabama. Jefferson County" in the bibliography. Sometimes you are dealing with a more specific office in a county government, which complicates this further.

While there could be several approaches here, I have chosen a method that creates the most readable form across all references. Create the entire jurisdiction information in the Last Name field. For U.S. jurisdictions, start with the state, and then put the county or parish name in parentheses. If there is an even more specific jurisdiction within the county, use two dashes or an em dash to separate them. If a jurisdiction begins with terms like "City of," put that at the end of the more distinctive name, with a comma separating the terms, to allow for the most effective sorting in alphabetical order.

Alabama (Jefferson County)
Alabama (Jefferson County—Birmingham, City of)
England (Cornwall—Week St. Mary)

This allows you to sort materials by state (or country), then county and smaller subset jurisdictions. If you chose instead to put the county name first, you might create confusion when numerous records beginning with "Jefferson County" sort together, while all from different states. Due to the way Zotero formats punctuation for the author of these references, the parentheses work better than periods to give you well-formatted footnotes and bibliographic entries.

If you are documenting a non-government institution as the creator of the material, you will begin with the name of the institution, putting the location in parentheses. All of this will be placed in the Last Name field. Example: Immaculate Conception Church (Natchitoches, Louisiana).

Artifacts

Zotero's *CMOS* style includes item types for things that have been written, published, presented, filmed, artistically rendered, and recorded. It does not have item types for artifacts other than artwork. I have found that the Manuscript item type in Zotero is often the best for handling artifacts in private hands. *EE* has a QuickCheck Model for Zella Stabler's scrapbook, suggesting these elements for the bibliographic citation:

QuickCheck Model from Evidence Explained, *p. 105*

In Zotero, I created a Zotero citation record with the following field data:

Item Type	Manuscript
Author	Stabler, Zella (Lovell)
Type	Scrapbook, ca. 1930–80, privately held by Mrs. Stabler
Date	2015
Archive	[address for private use*], Williamsport, Pennsylvania

*In your notes, you will store the real address of the person who holds the record, but you will delete it before publication.

Zotero will convert this data into the following bibliographic item:

Stabler, Zella (Lovell). Scrapbook, ca. 1930–80, privately held by Mrs. Stabler, 2015. Williamsport, Pennsylvania.

One thing to note about this particular arrangement: there is no formal title for this scrapbook. So, you are leaving the title field empty to get the optimal citation. However, your Research List will have an empty spot where you expect to see the key piece of information identifying an item. The item will still be findable with a search or by the Author field. But if the empty title is troublesome to you, put "n.t." for "not titled." You can choose to remove it when your bibliography and

Title	Creator	Date	Archive
	Bellevue Cemetery Office...		
	Stabler	2015	[address for p...
1850 United States Federal Census	Ancestry.com	2009	
Amish Friendship Sampler Album [ca. 187...	Horst and et al		Michigan Stat...
"Barbour Collection of Connecticut Vital ...	Barbour (comp) and Barb...		Connecticut S...
Cherokee Council Minutes, 1818 May 20 [...	University System of Geo...		

If you leave a title field empty, your Research List will reflect the empty field.

references have been created in your publication. But it is also acceptable to have "n.t" to indicate that an item was not formally titled.

Unwanted capitalization in title fields

Zotero attempts to perfect our exported citations by putting title fields into "title case" or "headline style." Sometimes you will not want the information capitalized, especially if you are using the field for a purpose other than the one for which it was designed.

You can circumvent the capitalization by putting something into the Language field that Zotero does not recognize as a language. If you put "English" here, or leave it blank with English as the default language in your preferences, Zotero assumes it should use the English-language practice of putting a title into title case.

I use "as typed" in the Language field to force it to leave the text exactly as I typed it. This hack does not work, unfortunately, on quotation marks around the field's contents. If you begin and end your title field's contents with quotation marks, Zotero will strip them out unless it is a field that requires quotation marks, like an article title.

Handling Derivatives

The *EE* recommendation that you cite the chain of evidence—acknowledging use of a derivative source or even a derivative of a derivative—creates a challenge for Zotero. Fortunately, though, even these most complex of citations can be stored in Zotero, even if they cannot be automatically exported fully publication-ready.

The key to doing these worrisome citations in the most worry-free way is to embed in the automated citation a pointer to any information you are having to store outside the normally used Zotero fields. The derivative history of a source usually appears at the reference note level and not in the source bibliography in *EE*. You can mimic *EE* format using one of several methods. We will walk through all three with the same reference, which appears on page 617 of *EE*, the section titled "Online Databases with Images." Here is the bibliographic entry and the reference note, as presented by *EE*.

Source List Entry

"Freedman's Bank Records, 1865–1871." Database with images. Ancestry.com. http://www.ancestry.com: 2015.

First Reference Note

1. "Freedman's Bank Records, 1865–1871," images, Ancestry .com (http://www.ancestry.com: 1 April 2015), Mrs. Zelphire Edwards, bank card no. 696 (bank not identified but context suggests the New Orleans branch); citing "Registers of Signatures of Depositors in Branches of the Freedman's Savings and Trust Company, 1865–1874, M816, 27 rolls" (exact roll not cited, but should be 11).

Method 1: Zotero format with derivatives in Extra field

This source is database at a website, so we will use the Book Section item type. The Edition field holds the type of source, and a placeholder reference to the derivative material, which we store in the Extra field. (For other item types, replace the Edition field with Type or other fields that allow free-form entry of information.) The information in Extra will be added as citation detail, when creating the first footnote or endnote in a publication. Here are the Zotero fields used and their contents:

Item Type	Book Section
Title	Freedman's Bank Records, 1865–1871
Book Title	Ancestry.com
Edition	database with images; [see Extra]
URL	http://www.ancestry.com
Accessed	4/1/2015
Extra	Mrs. Zelphire Edwards, bank card no. 696 (bank not identified but context suggests the New Orleans branch); citing "_Registers of Signatures of Depositors in Branches of the Freedman's Savings and Trust Company, 1865–1874_, M816, 27 rolls" (exact roll not cited, but should be 11). EE617

The benefit of this method lies in the fact that all of your detail is in one view. The limitation lies in the fact that the Extra field is not a rich-text field. You will need to flag any italicized phrases by underscores at each end of the affected text, as you see above.

Also note that I have put "EE617" at the end of the text in the Extra field. This tells me that the rules about this citation can be found in my *EE* book on page 617.

Zotero's formatted citation for this will be simple:

"Freedman's Bank Records, 1865–1871," in *Ancestry.com*, database with images [see Extra], accessed April 1, 2015, http://www.ancestry.com.

The phrase "[see Extra]" is your reminder that you need to draw the citation detail and derivative material from the Extra field. You will remove the "[see Extra]" note and paste the contents of Extra (except "EE617") after the original citation, adapting punctuation, as required. The final citation will look like this:

> "Freedman's Bank Records, 1865–1871," in *Ancestry.com*, database with images, accessed April 1, 2015, http://www.ancestry.com; Mrs. Zelphire Edwards, bank card no. 696 (bank not identified but context suggests the New Orleans branch); citing "*Registers of Signatures of Depositors in Branches of the Freedman's Savings and Trust Company, 1865–1874*, M816, 27 rolls" (exact roll not cited, but should be 11).

Method 2: Store citation detail in notes

In cases where you will be citing this same major source multiple times for different ancestors, you might prefer Method 2. In this

Freedman's Bank Records, 1865–1871
Zelphire Edwards Notes

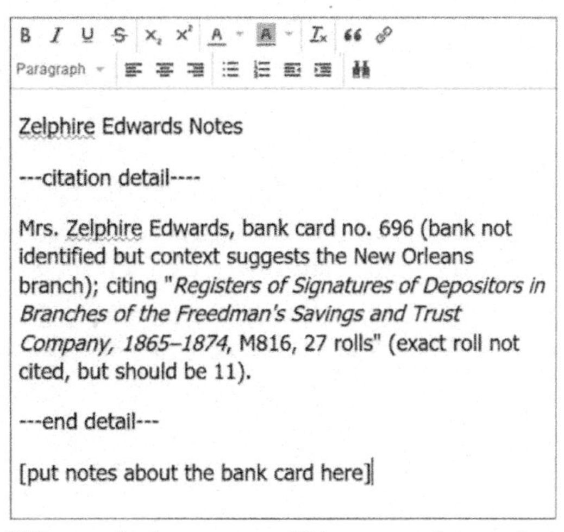

When multiple ancestors will have notes from a single source, you may create a note per ancestor and keep the citation detail information at this level.

method, you will set up the main Zotero record as described in Method 1, except you will put "[See notes for citation detail and derivative information]" note in Edition. While you do not have to place detail in the Extra field, you might want to store the information there anyway, as the template for the citation detail you will store in each note.

You will attach notes to this Zotero record for each ancestor you find in the source. In this case, you would start with a note about Zelphire Edwards. Within the note, you need to include the citation detail you would add to this source, when citing anything about this particular ancestor. And, of course, capitalizing on Zotero's power to file information in multiple locations, you will also drag the note into Zelphire Edwards's PEOPLE file.

Method 3: Free-form entry note in *EE* format

If you want your final *EE*-ready footnote created, formatted, and ready to paste wherever you need it, you can create a very simple Zotero entry with only the most basic information. Then add a note, labeling it "Free-form EE format." Create the reference citation in the attached note, following *EE* style perfectly.

Personally, I prefer to wait until I know which reference notes I am going to need in a publication before I perfect the form. And I like to have my Zotero information complete. But then again, you can do both—fill in Zotero fully and create a perfected note.

Summary

While this might seem complex at first, you will soon find that you can quickly translate the *EE* formats to a satisfactory Zotero equivalent, in most cases. You will find that your Zotero-generated citations give you the materials and nearly the form for publication in venues that require *EE* perfection. It will grow easier with every attempt.

Now, let's look at two other standard tools of genealogy that Zotero can replace: research logs and to-do lists.

RESEARCH LOGS & TO-DO LISTS 13

Research logs and to-do lists have long been staples of the genealogy toolkit. They have changed forms many times—their purpose and best practices debated. The last thing many of you will want to hear is yet another zealot preaching a change to your system. But I will. Apostasy it may be, but Zotero replaces your research log and your to-do list, bringing those old ideas to new levels of efficiency.

RESEARCH LOGS

I know how sacred we have made the tomes we call research logs. And I suppose, in a diary sense, they are the stories of our genealogical lives. What they are *not* is efficient. Even if you have yours on OneNote, fully searchable, you are wasting time. Sacrilege, I know, but I must call it as I see it.

The primary purpose of research logs has been to keep a record of what we have searched, so we do not repeat the effort. Back when all of our records were on paper, nonportable, the research log was the concise and somewhat portable record and the fastest way to remind yourself of what had been done before. It made beautiful and perfect sense in a world of index cards and manila folders.

Once your full body of research is available everywhere you go—as Zotero makes possible—a log makes no sense. Your record of what you have searched should be attached to the research itself, now that the research is fully portable.

Zotero's answer to the research log

Let's get specific about what the typical research log has and how Zotero replaces it. A research log might track this information:

- Date of research
- Repository
- Call number
- Source citation
- Scope of search
- Results
- File ID

I have seen some research logs with a slightly different setup, useful as a to-do list. We will deal with that in the last part of this chapter.

Rather than organizing your research around the date order in which you did things (of dubious importance), Zotero organizes all you need to know around the sources you consulted. As to the items above, here is why Zotero replaces everything you need.

Date of research

Quite honestly, unless you are billing someone or you are dealing with a malleable source like a database or website, I do not see why you need to know the date of your research. But you certainly can track it in Zotero, if needed. Zotero will capture two dates for you automatically—the date you first create a source record and the last time you modified it. If it is important to you to know exactly when you got a specific piece of information, type it into the notes. In fact you can put a note under each source that is a "_Record of Source Consultation," with an underscore to drive it always to the top of all that source record's notes.

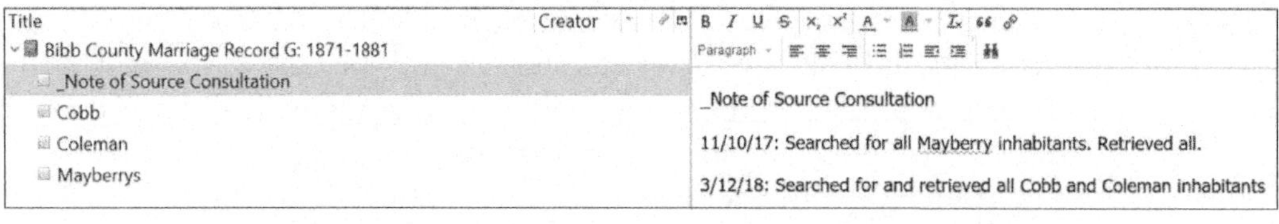

If you need to know exactly when you consulted a source, keep a consultation note under the source or put dates in your actual notes about the record.

Repository, call number, and source citation

These are standard fields on your research record. And because Zotero is structured data, you are far less likely to leave out a critical piece of information.

Scope of search and results

It should be our standard practice as we take any notes in Zotero to identify what we were searching for and what we found in any given record. You may do it in the consultation note described above. Better yet, though, do it as part of your research notes. I often find myself searching a number of surnames while I am in a single source. I make a note of each surname, as you see in the image above. The first thing I put in the note is a quick message to myself about what I searched for. Was I looking for every person with that surname in the record, or did I only look at one or two specific names? When I encounter this source again, I can quickly see in Zotero that I have been here before. And in the notes, I can determine if I have more work to do here.

File ID

You no longer need to create a system of matching your research log to the photocopies you bring home from a research trip. Even if you bring home paper, scan it and attach all relevant scans to the source record in Zotero. But if you find you must keep a piece of paper, you can still put an ID number into your Zotero record, in the Extra field.

What about your old logs?

To those who still have the room full of paper and will never in this lifetime get it all into Zotero: You will still need the old research logs, yes. Digitize them, if you have not already, and pull them into Zotero. If they are typed, OCR the records so they become searchable.

Let all your new research happen without logs.

To-do lists

Most family tree software tools offer an embedded to-do list feature—useful, as far as they go. Unfortunately, most do not go far enough. Many are not accessible away from your own computer. If you have to move or restore your data via GEDCOM, you risk losing your to-do items. Most tools are not designed to let you apply a single to-do item to multiple people or projects. Zotero, on the other hand, provides the ideal research to-do list, simply by being itself. It fully integrates with research notes, reduces repetitious work, and goes anywhere.

I have created a to-do list in Zotero by creating a collection where I drop items I need to handle. I like my to-do lists to fall at the top of my Zotero library menu, so I have named my collection "_RESEARCH TO-DO LIST," beginning with the underscore character to make it fall first in alphabetical order. Items on my family history to-do list typically fall into one of these three categories:

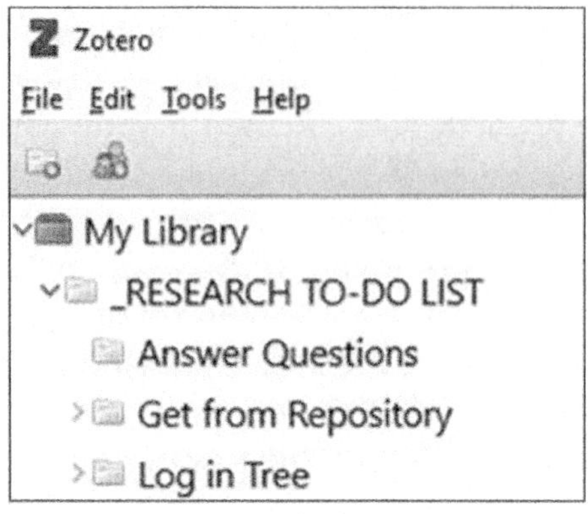

Use the Zotero Collections to create your desired to-do organization.

- Research needed to answer a question about an ancestor or group of them
- Records or books I want to review the next time I go to a particular repository or that I need to order
- Things I have already collected and now need to process into my tree software

You might find that a different organizational structure suits your research practices better. But I have created three subfolders—Answer Questions, Get from Repository, and Log in Tree—to hold the to-do items in each category.

Answer questions

As we work through the data on our ancestors, we inevitably encounter problems that need analysis. We might not have the time or records to analyze the questions immediately. But we want to make sure we do it when possible.

For such issues, I create a note—a to-do item for the specific ancestor or group. In the example below, you see an entry for Michael Mayberry. It displays my notes to myself of problems with birth and death dates that need resolution.

Another value of Zotero lies in the ability it gives us to drag a single item into multiple folders. In doing this, it exists only once but can be seen wherever it is of use. In the Michael Mayberry example, this entry also sits in the "Michael Mayberry" folder in my PEOPLE collection.

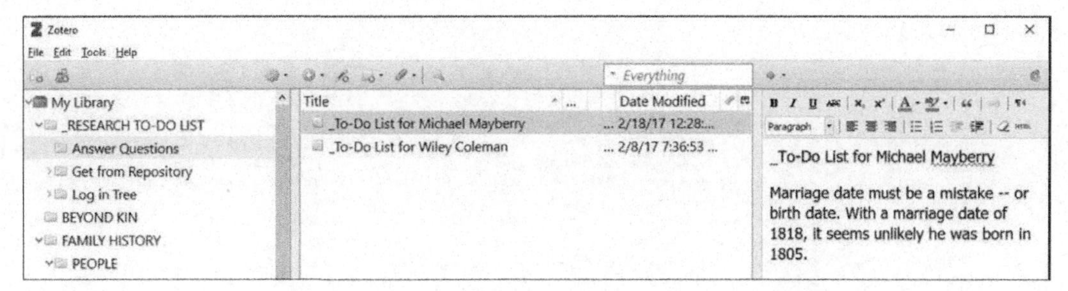

Questions needing answers are gathered in the "Answer Questions" folder and can simultaneously be stored in other relevant folders. Unlike traditional paper systems, your research is filed away in the appropriate place and in the "to-do" stack at the same time.

Regardless of whether you find this entry by way of the to-do list, through Michael Mayberry's folder, or through a search, any change you make is changing it everywhere. The up-to-date record appears no matter what folder you found it in.

I also believe strongly in the power of a research plan, digging deeply into a question and how you plan to answer it. My own GEG Research Plan design is available online at https://goldenchannel-publishing.com/shop/ if you have not yet found a favorite. You will likely create your research plan in Microsoft Word or another tool of choice. But store a link to it in your to-do folder for the ancestor. So the minute you are ready to pick up the next task in your basket, you can get straight to the plan.

Get from repository

A great value of Zotero lies in its ability to extract bibliographic information from web pages, especially library catalogs, through the Zotero Connector (see Chapter 7). Our to-do lists are, often as not, a tickler to check out a particular resource the next time we are able to go to a specific library or archive. Zotero can grab everything you need to find a record, organize it by the archive in which it can be found, and then become the record in which you take notes and cite the source.

Under my *Get from Repository* collection, I have a folder for any archive or collection I might need to visit or consult. I gather records here of every source that interests me. When I have the time at last to visit an archive, I have the research list ready to go.

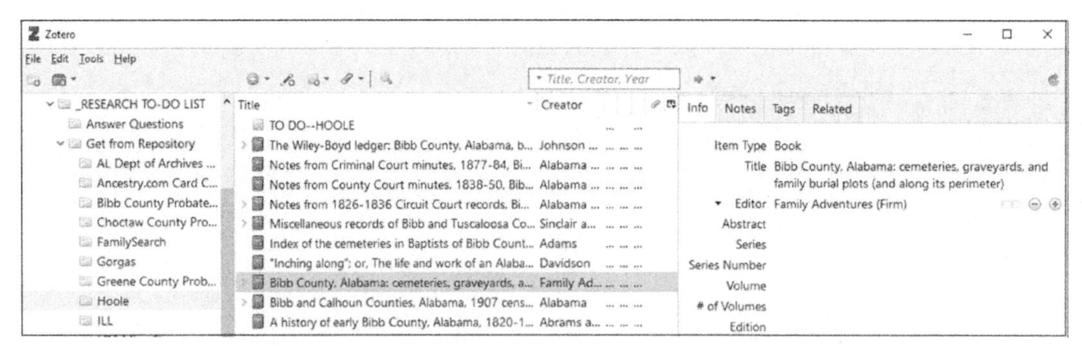

The Zotero Connector capture of bibliographic references from websites creates a quick method of identifying sources to be consulted when visiting repositories.

In this example, I have created a repository folder called "Hoole." In it, I am collecting a list of potentially useful sources from the catalog of the W. S. Stanley Hoole Special Collections Library at the University of Alabama. On the Hoole website, I see a book about Bibb County cemeteries that could answer a question about a particular ancestor. Zotero Connector populates the bibliographic information in the Detail pane with one click.

I also drag the entry into a folder for Bibb County, Alabama, in my PLACES collection, where it will remain permanently, long after it ceases to be a "to do." To this record, I will add research notes and attach PDFs of any pages I scan.

Since Zotero syncs data to its own cloud, I can get to my repository to-do list from any Internet-connected computer. If I find myself able to visit a repository unexpectedly with no time to print out to-do lists or to pack my laptop, I still know exactly what I intended to do at this archive. I can take the notes in Zotero's online environment and sync them back to my desktop software, ready for me when I get home.

Log in tree

Once the research has been done in a repository, you have to extract relevant details from the repository research into your family trees, using your genealogy software of choice. Zotero allows you to keep a virtual in-box of data awaiting transcription, extraction, and updating.

I have two subfolders in this collection, one called "Folder in Progress" and one called "To Do Eventually." While most of my work sits directly in the "Log in Tree" folder, these other two help me to organize priorities. The "Folder in Progress" reminds me where I left off,

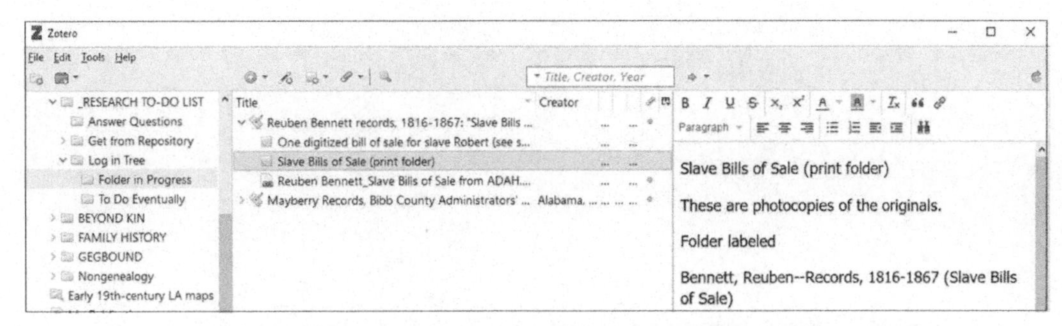

Research notes can be dropped into the Log in Tree folder--or one of its subfolders--awaiting processing into the family tree. Meanwhile the data can also be filed in its permanent folders.

last time I worked on extracting research notes. The "To Do Eventually" folder is where I drop items that are of a lower priority, so I put my attention where it most needs to be.

When you do your research on paper, the photocopies and research notes you bring home from an archive can sit in a box for months and years, waiting for you to extract them. While they sit there, you cannot easily find them, if you remember you have them at all.

In Zotero, you can take all these pending items and drag them into proper folders — places, people, and other topical folders — so that your filing is up to date, long before you have properly processed the data.

Summary

While Zotero developers did not design it to be a to-do list or research log, it easily becomes these, with the creation of a few folders. Better, it becomes so much more than either of these could ever be in their traditional forms. It creates something even better than our more recently elected forms like Microsoft Word, OneNote, Evernote and your tree software. It integrates all your work together in the optimal way.

Next, I will wrap up with a few more great things Zotero offers us in genealogy.

MORE OF ZOTERO FOR GENEALOGY

14

As we approach the end of this book, I do not pretend to have covered all that can be known about Zotero. An entire book could be written, no doubt, on methods to create and edit Zotero styles alone. But before we depart, there are a few more things I want to show you.

ZOTERO ON THE ROAD

Zotero's ability to travel well stands as one of its most useful features. You can access everything you are syncing to Zotero's cloud storage from a remote location if you have a computer with Internet access.

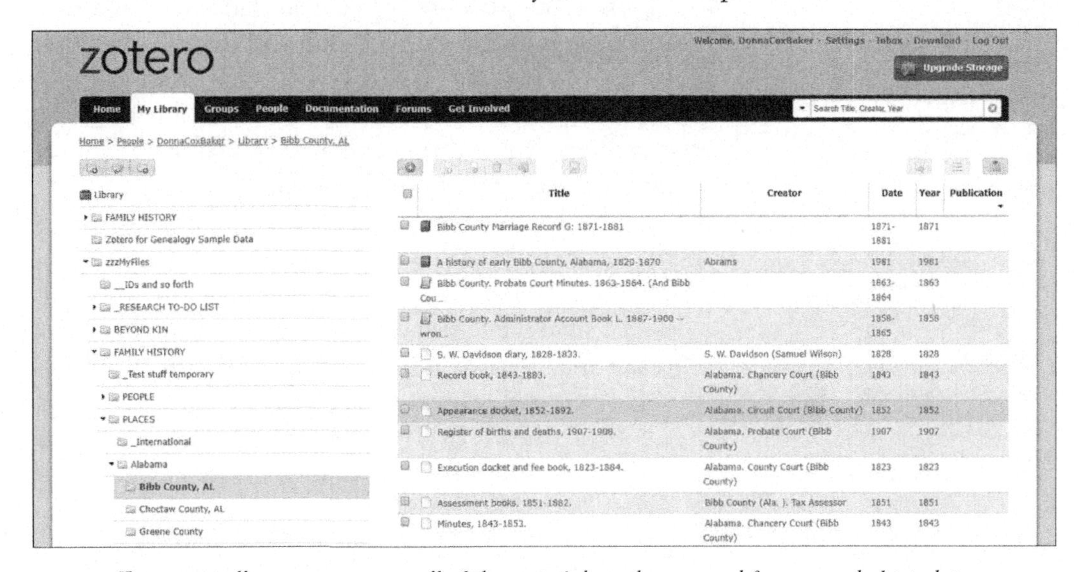

Zotero.org allows you to access all of the material you have synced from your desktop data.

As we discussed in Chapter 5, you have the choice of embedding your attachments into Zotero or linking to them externally. If you chose to embed them, the attachments will be available to you when you log in to the online version of Zotero. The ability to read the attachments, of course, depends on whether the computer you are using has the appropriate software for the particular attachment (Word, Excel, etc.).

If you linked to attachments outside of Zotero, you will not be able to open them from the online Zotero interface on someone else's computer. However, if you are storing your attachments in a cloud environment (as I recommend), you will be able to find and open them that way (again, assuming you have the appropriate software on the computer you are using remotely).

Using Zotero's online environment and the cloud for attachments, you can have all of your research notes with you, with no effort. You don't even have to plan. It is there.

Edit in a Separate Window

When you get ready to take notes in Zotero, you often need to display something else on the screen at the same time. Zotero allows you to detach a note into a separate and sizable window, for placement wherever it is convenient for your notetaking. I mentioned this feature in Chapter 3, but I wanted to give it a bit more attention.

In a Zotero note, when you click the **Edit in a separate window** button, Zotero extracts your notes to a free-standing window with your editing tools. You can resize the window and move it anywhere on the screen you find useful. It will also allow you to open multiple windows at the same time.

This is particularly helpful if you are taking notes from a website or other application also displayed on your screen. It allows you to move the bulk of Zotero out of sight while you continue to take notes. You can make the notes window narrow and tall, short and wide, or a small square in a corner.

This feature is also useful if you are consulting your notes while working in other software. Let's say

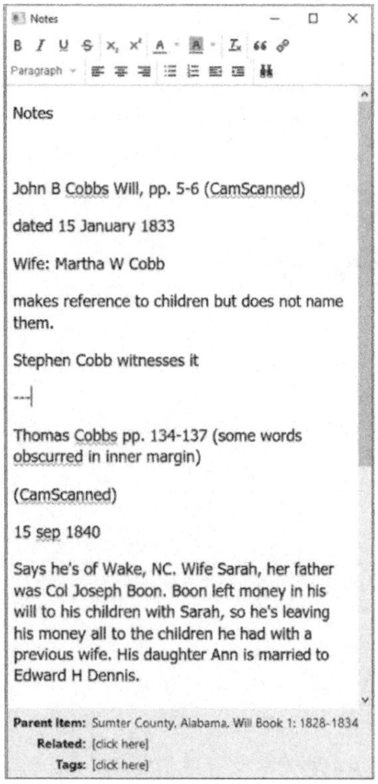

Zotero allows you to open your notes in sizable, movable windows, moving them into available space around other tools.

you are writing an article or book, based on your research. This allows you to have your word-processing software open over much of your screen, with your research displayed in as tight a space as you need.

Transcribing manuscripts

As genealogists, we often find ourselves transcribing old handwritten documents. You can transcribe them directly into Zotero notes in the freestanding window. This creates a fully searchable document where there was once just a graphic of handwriting. Both the manuscript scan and the transcription can be attachments to the Zotero citation.

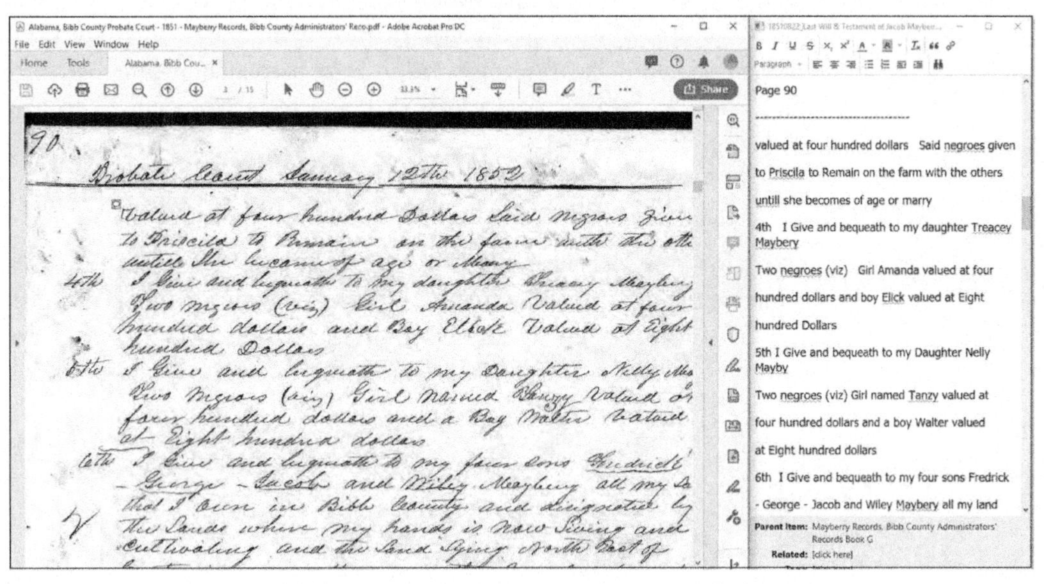

Zotero becomes your manuscript transcription tool when you choose to edit your note in a separate window.

Collaborating and Sharing

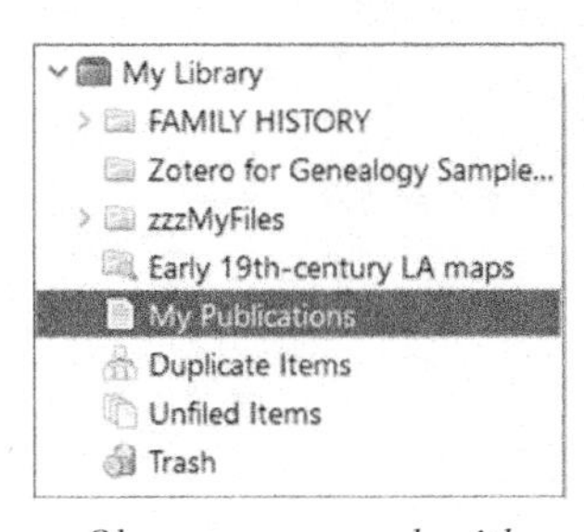

Share your research with anyone by using My Publications.

Zotero allows you to share bibliographies or your research with others. You can share it generally, with open public accessibility, or specifically within a defined group.

My Publications

If you are creating work you want (and have the right) to share with the public generally, you can drag the Zotero items into a folder in your Collections pane

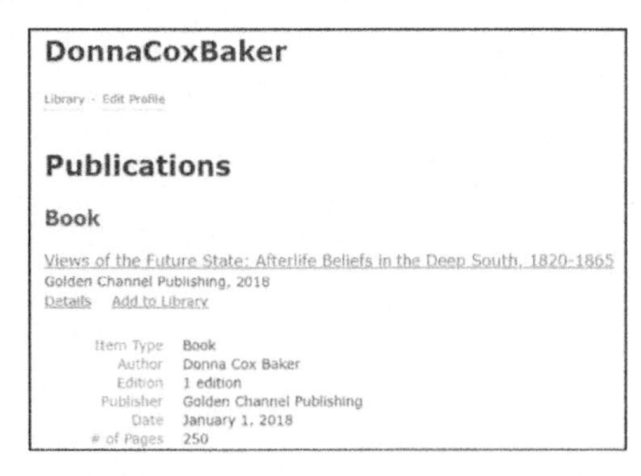

My Publications creates a list of your work with open public access.

called "My Publications." This would be an excellent place to make a copy of a one-of-a-kind source available widely.

The items will form a bibliography on your profile page on Zotero.org. You may use the Abstract field to annotate them, and you can add PDFs. Zotero will place the responsibility fully and consciously on you to ensure you have the right to publish anything you upload. You will be asked to confirm it before Zotero accepts it.

If you do not want this information to be viewed on your profile page, adjust the privacy settings on the profile. You can choose to suppress notes or to let your entire library be viewable.

Groups

Zotero offers you a facility to create groups around a specific interest. For genealogists, groups can be useful to tie together the research of those working on a similar family. You were introduced to a group when you began to work on the exercises for this book. In joining the

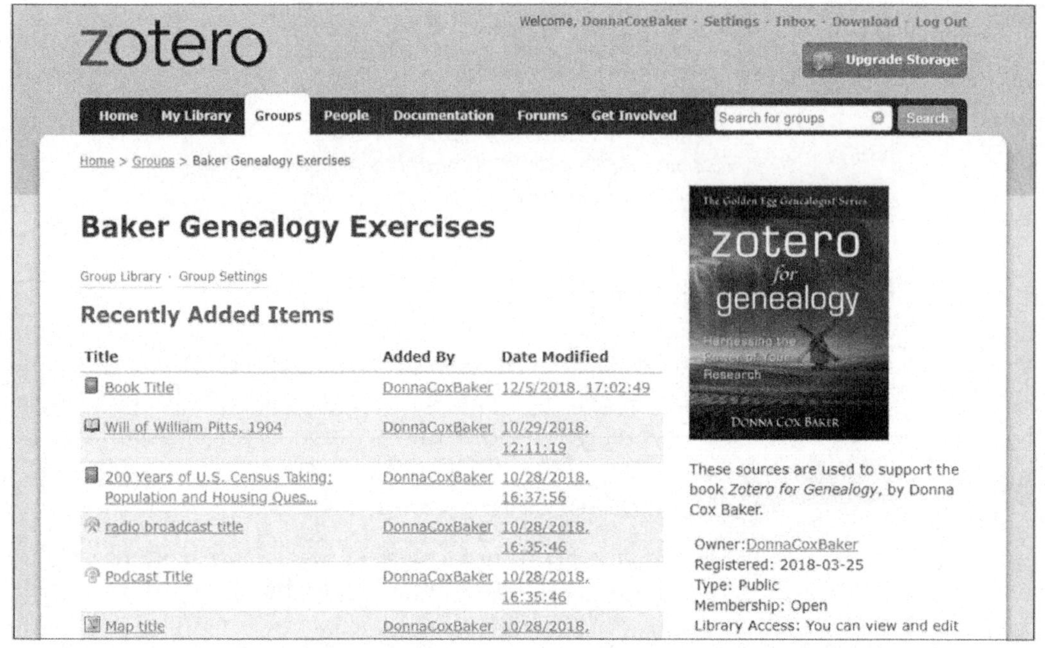

Your Zotero Group Library allows those of like interest or a shared mission to collaborate and discuss their research.

Baker Genealogy Exercises group, material I had added to a group library showed up in your Zotero workspace.

You create a group by logging into Zotero.org and choosing the Group menu option. Click **Create a New Group**. You will then give your group a name and set up the privacy options you prefer. You can then update the Library Settings to determine whether who can do what to the material in your Group Library.

If you choose to create a group that lets others contribute, multiple people could add items to a library in your *Group Libraries* section of your Collections pane. You can control the rights of group members as a whole or individually using Member Settings. If you choose to let others add to the library, it will count toward your storage limits—so be prepared for that.

OTHER BIBLIOGRAPHIC SOFTWARE—IMPORTS AND EXPORTS

Zotero can import and export data to and from many of the major bibliographic software products. You can import an entire research set—whatever has been saved into the importable file—or you may import a single item from the clipboard.

For exports, you may choose whether notes and attachments will be included with the bibliographic data. You can export as a collection or the entire library. You may choose to export it as a Zotero RDF file, to save as a backup. It can be a comma-separated value (CSV) file. It can export to EndNote, RefWorks, Evernote, and Wikipedia. Many other options expand the number of products Zotero can export to.

WRAPPING UP

I hope this book has encouraged you to try Zotero. As your research and notetaking tool, it offers so much more than many tools I have tried. Even as I prepared to write this book, I kept discovering new features. I trust you will have the same experience. Zotero has been my tool of choice for nearly a decade now. That it happens to be free, well that's just a nice bonus. Enjoy your Zotero journey!

Visit our website and forum at
zoteroforgenealogy.com

INDEX

abstract field, 44, 132
Accessed, 118
add-ons, 3, 6, 9, 16, 23, 66, 67, 72, 74, 81, 82, 83, 84, 85, 86, 88, 91
Alfred P. Sloan Foundation, xiii
Andrew W. Mellon Foundation, xiii
annotations, 74, 77, 78, 79
archives, 112, 116
articles, 65, 104
artifacts, 110, 115
artwork, 115
attachments, 8, 16, 18, 34, 49, 50, 51, 52, 53, 55, 56, 57, 97, 130, 131, 133
  broken links, 57
  embedded v. linked, 18, 50, 56
  searchable, 52
audio files, 3, 49
authors, 26, 55, 61, 112, 115, 116
backing up data, 50
Baker Genealogy Exercises, 19, 133
Balderson, Linda, xiii
base directory, 52, 53
bibliographic software, 133
bibliography, 81, 82, 84, 89, 102, 103, 104, 131, 132
Big-R Research, 3
book section, 103
bookmarklet, 69
books, xv, 8, 9, 20, 21, 24, 25, 28, 30, 31, 38, 55, 65, 70, 71, 72, 74, 85, 93, 101, 102, 103, 126, 129, 131, 132, 133, 139
call number, 122, 123
capitalization, 117
chain of evidence, 107, 110
Chicago Manual of Style, 2, 6, 23, 25, 26, 81, 82, 84, 87, 90, 105, 110, 111
Chrome, 69, 70
citation preview, 105
citations, xv, 2, 5, 6, 8, 9, 15, 16, 23, 24, 25, 26, 28, 31, 32, 34, 53, 56, 62, 70, 75, 81, 82, 84, 85, 86, 88, 105, 107, 108, 112
  attachments, 53, 56
  corrections, 87
  creation, 6, 15, 25, 28, 31, 85, 86, 87
  derivatives, 110
  detail, 88, 89, 102
  fact-level, 4
  language, 84
  multiple, 86, 87, 88
  one or many, 101, 102, 103, 104
  research log, 122, 123
  software tools, 3, 6
  storage in word processor, 85
  style, 23, 24, 84, 107, 108
  type, 24, 25, 26
  updates, 85
  URLs, 55
  word processing, 85
cloud storage, 8, 16, 17, 18, 50, 52, 56, 75, 126, 129, 130
Coffman, Dorothy Yoder, 3
collaboration, 4, 7, 131
collectible items, 49

collections, 6, 42, 43, 76, 124
creation, 42, 43
deleting, 46
exporting, 133
organization, 42, 95
pane, 15, 19, 24, 34, 37, 41, 43, 44, 55, 57, 64, 65, 66, 76, 131, 133
records, 44, 45, 46
searching, 64
sorting, 59, 60
subcollections, 46, 64, 70, *See* collections
to-do list, 124
columns, 59, 60, 61
comma-separated values file, 133
comments, xv, 77, 78
contributor, 26
converting old paper system to Zotero, 4
copying folders, 46
Corporation for Digital Scholarship, xiii
creator, 61, 63
date, 116
dates, 27, 29, 60, 63, 104, 122, 124
dates as timeline, 104
deleting collections, 46
deleting research item, 34
derivatives, 110, 117
details, research, 15, 24, 25, 29, 31, 32, 35, 78
edit in a separate window. See notes
edition, 29, 118
editor, 26
PDFs, 78
EndNote, 133
endnotes, 6, 84, 85, 87
error reporting, 21
EverNote, 2, 6, 127, 133
Evidence Explained, 2, 6, 28, 31, 55, 81, 106, 107, 108, 109, 110, 111, 115, 120
challenges with computer databases, 109
Kindle, 110, 113
QuickCheck Models, 108
exporting and importing, 133
Extra field, 118, 123
Family Tree Maker, 3
family tree software, 3, 4, 123, 124
file ID, 122, 123
files
organization, 53
relocating, 52
filing, multiple, 5, 44
Firefox, 69
font displays, 35
footnotes, xvi, 6, 84, 85, 86, 87, 88, 89
forums, 20
free-form citation entry, 120
GEG Research Plan, 125
George Mason University, xiii, 1
Golden Egg Genealogists, 2
Group Libraries, 19, 133
groups, 19, 131, 132
help, 20
highlights, 32, 77
HTML format, 32
images, 3
installation, 13
Institute for Genealogy and Historical Research, xiii
Institute of Museum and Library Services, xiii
item types, 24, 25, 61, 88, 103, 111
book, 26, 112
book section, 27, 118
interview, 27
letter, 27
Language field, 117
Last Name, 115
Legacy Family Tree, 3
Legewie, Joscha, 67, 73
library catalog, 31, 70, 125
LibreOffice, 6, 81, 82, 85
Linux, 8, 13
local jurisdiction as creator, 115
macOS, 8
Manuscript item type, 116
maps, 50, 65
member settings, 133
metadata, 31, 38, 72
Microsoft Office, 8
Microsoft Windows, 8
Microsoft Word, 6, 32, 33, 52, 82, 84, 85, 91, 125, 127
military personnel record, 26
Mills, Elizabeth Shown, 28, 55, 107
moving folders, 46
music, 49

My Library, 15, 20, 24, 34, 42, 43, 44, 45, 46, 59, 64, 65, 66, 70
My Publications, 132
newspapers, 104
Newspapers.com, 104
notes, xv, 3, 5, 8, 15, 23, 29, 31, 34, 55, 84, 98, 99, 101, 104, 122, 124, 125, 126, 130, 131, 132, 133
PDF comments, 74
creation, 32
extracting, 127
formatting, 35
images, 50
organization, 102, 103
pane, 33
PDF comments, 73, 77, 78
PDF highlights, 73, 74, 77, 78
remote accessibility, 130
scope of research, 123
searching, 62, 63
separate window, 33
separate window, 33
separate window, 130
to-do lists, 124
OneNote, 2, 4, 6, 121, 127
open source software, 3, 67
Optical Character Recognition (OCR), 52, 123
organization
files, 96
organization, files, 52, 95
panes, resizing, 36
paperless genealogy, 3
PDF, searchable, 51
PDFs, xv, 16, 49, 51, 52, 56, 62, 67, 74, 75, 76, 77, 78, 79, 126, 132
searchable, 52, 56, 73, 77
PEOPLE collection, 43, 53, 96, 97
photographs, 49
place field, 26
PLACES collection, 53, 97, 98, 126
portability, 7
preferences, 3, 16, 23, 35, 52, 74, 75, 76, 78, 79, 82, 84
previewing citation styles, 105
publisher, 26, 29, 109
Publisher field, 112
QuickCheck Model, 115
quotation marks, 117
reading stack, 73, 74, 75, 76, 79
record of source consultation, 122
RefWorks, 133
related records, 38, 39
relative path, 52, 53, 57
relocating files, 52
remote access, 17, 50, 129
removing items, 45
reports, 85
repository, 122, 123, 124, 125
research list, 15, 24, 25, 28, 31, 32, 34, 35, 44, 45, 53, 55, 59, 60, 61, 66, 75, 77, 79, 103, 105, 125
pane, 37
Research List, 116
research logs, xvi, 5, 6, 121, 122, 123, 127
research plan, 125
research, detail, 126
Richardson, Emily, xiii, 3
rich-text format, 32, 52
Rochester, Blake, xiii
RootsMagic, 3
Roy Rosenzweig Center for History and New Media, xiii, xvi, 1
Safari, 69
sample data. See Zotero for Genealogy Sample Data
scope of search, 123
searching, 4, 51, 61, 62, 66, 98
advanced, 62
saved, 64, 65
series editor, 26
sharing, 131
short citations, 114
Smith, Adam, xiii
sorting, 27, 59, 60, 61, 115
sorting folders, 42, 46
spreadsheets, 3, 4, 49, 52
stacked view, 35
standard view, 35
Stillman, Dan, xiii
storage needs, 50, 56
style manager, 82, 105
style preview, 105, 111
style standards, 16, 90, 108
surname files, 53, 96

syncing data, 13, 16, 18, 50, 56, 129
tags, 15, 16, 37, 38, 62, 63, 66
text files, 49, 51, 56, 62
Title, 118
titles, 29, 55, 61, 104
to-do lists, xvi, 6, 121, 122, 123, 124, 125, 126, 127
TOOLS collection, 53, 98
TOPICS collection, 53, 99
transcribing manuscripts, 131
translator, 27
trash bin, 34, 45, 46
troubleshooting, 20
Tuscaloosa Genealogical Society, xiii
Type field, 113
type-ahead feature, 26
types, 116
untitled works, 116
updating software, 21
URI links, 54, 55
URL, 118
URLs, 16, 23, 26, 28, 54, 55, 57, 70, 82
user interface, 35
videos, 3
volume, 112
Wikipedia, 133
Windows, 81
word processing, 16, 51, 81, 82, 83, 85
workspace, 8, 14, 16, 30, 33, 35, 36, 41, 66, 105, 133
modifying, 35
WorldCat, 31
year, 61
Zotero (defined), 2
Zotero account, 17, 21
Zotero Bibliographic Formats, 20, 111
Zotero cloud, 16, 18, 50, 56, 126, 129
Zotero Connector, 31, 38, 67, 69, 70, 71, 72, 125, 126
Zotero for Genealogy Sample Data, 20, 21, 24, 28, 42, 43, 44, 45, 55, 56, 57, 61, 65, 76
Zotero online, 19, 130, 132, 133
Zotero online documentation, 20
Zotero profile, 132
Zotero RDF, 133
Zotero Word Processor Plug-in, 67
ZotFile, 67, 72, 73, 74, 75, 76, 77, 78, 79

About the Author

Donna Cox Baker began her writing and editing career in technical communications for a Fortune 500 computer corporation. Discovering a passion for genealogy and history, she made a move into historical publishing in 2002 and earned a PhD in history. She authored *Views of the Future State: Afterlife Beliefs in the Deep South, 1820–1865*, published in 2018. She works in magazine and book publishing and manages her own blog about family history at the *Golden Egg Genealogist* (gegbound.com). She cofounded the *Beyond Kin Project* (beyondkin.org), which encourages the descendants of slaveholders to take up the mission of documenting the whole plantation—black and white. Her early days in the computer industry created in her a desire to find better, faster, and more efficient ways to get things done. She is particularly interested in eliminating wasted time and effort in the field of genealogy. She considers Zotero a critical part of that mission.

The Golden Egg Genealogist

Manifesting the treasures of ancestry. A shared journey.

gegbound.com

The Beyond Kin Project

For every soul a story, a family, a name.

beyondkin.org

goldenchannelpublishing.com

Views of the Future State

Afterlife Beliefs in the Deep South, 1820–1865

Views of the Future State examines shifting conceptions of the afterlife among literate inhabitants of the antebellum and Civil War–era Deep South. The relatively static 1820 views of a dualistic heaven and hell took on a vibrant complexity by 1865. The challenges of scientific discoveries, universalism, mesmerism, spiritualism, Swedenborgianism, and finally war encouraged bold questioning. Southerners no longer focused primarily on how to get to heaven, as they had done for generations. The seekers among them thirsted for detailed depictions of the celestial realms. They were particularly intrigued with those who claimed to have first-hand experience of heaven.

Afterlife beliefs then, as now, encompassed a complex and dynamic spectrum of thought. Baker begins to offer shape to the spectrum by examining the outer fringes of acceptable questioning—the place where orthodox religious people actively resisted deviations in thought and method by the seekers and skeptics in their midst.

Analyzing the voluminous writings of this era and the evidence of public consumption of and debate over them, Baker takes readers on a fascinating human journey. *Views of the Future State* presents a much-needed chapter in the heritage of spiritual seekers and raises timeless questions about life after death.

by

Donna Cox Baker

2018 250 pp.
8 B&W figures
978-0-9996899-0-5

Printed in Great Britain
by Amazon